# THE GLORY AND THE SHAME

By the same author:
  *Streams of Renewal*
  *One Lord One Spirit One Body*
  *Dictionary of the Pentecost and Charismatic Movements*
    (Editor)

# THE GLORY AND THE SHAME

Reflections on the 20th-Century
Outpouring of the Holy Spirit

## Peter Hocken

**Eagle**
Guildford, Surrey

Copyright © 1994 Peter Hocken

British Library Cataloguing-in-Publication Data. A catalogue record for
this book is available from the British Library

Published by Eagle, an imprint of Inter Publishing Service (IPS) Ltd, 59
Woodbridge Road, Guildford, Surrey GU1 4RF.

Typeset by The Electronic Book Factory Ltd, Fife, Scotland.
Printed in the UK by HarperCollins Manufacturing, Glasgow.

ISBN: 0 86347 117 X

# Contents

# FOREWORD

The Brighton Conference of 1991 brought together thousands of charismatic Christians from across the globe. It was unusual for many reasons, not least for having a conference within a conference. This inner conference comprised theologians within the charismatic movement. And modestly, graciously, thoughtfully organising and caring for them was a Roman Catholic priest, Dr. Peter Hocken. That is where he and I met.

And now he has asked me to write a word about his new book, and I am particularly thrilled to do so. It is an absolutely outstanding book, tracing as it does the glory and the shame of the charismatic movement throughout this century. But it is a work of theology rather than mere history. Here is a writer who is thoroughly at home with the wide spread of theology to be found in the Roman Catholic, Orthodox, Reformation and Pentecostal Churches. He knows and loves many of their leaders personally. And he is well aware of the growing phenomenon of the New Churches. I know of no book which gives such a balanced, warm, and deep perspective on the whole Christian scene since the remarkable outpouring of the Holy Spirit at the beginning of this century.

Why is this book so outstanding? Several reasons have suggested themselves to me.

*First, its breadth.*

As you read its pages you become aware of a man who is profoundly theological but can express it with simplicity; a man who has an astonishing breadth in his sympathies. The balance between the spiritual and the physical in God's dealings with us, the old and the new covenants, the corporate and the individual aspects, the institutional and what he calls the 'invasive' – when God breaks in: all this unfolds before us as we read, and it seems to be so clear and so obvious that we wonder why we did not see it before. That is the mark of great teaching.

*Second, its experience.*

Most scholars write from solitary desks. He writes out of a throbbing community. Most scholars who write about the Pentecostal phenomenon or the charismatic graces are not deeply experiencing the things of which they write. He is. This book breathes the wisdom of the sage and the dynamic spirituality of one who is on tip-toe for God to keep breaking in.

*Third, its dimensions.*

It puts the work of the Holy Spirit in the context of Christian unity on the one hand and the parousia on the other. Rarely have I met a theologian who sees all God's charisms in the light of Christ's return. Rarely do you find one who brings into the discussion a Messianic Judaism which declines to be assimilated into any of the denominations of Gentile Christianity. But it, too, is a sign of the Spirit's work and an anticipation of the End time.

*Fourth, its provenance*:

From a convinced Roman Catholic, who refuses the usual attitudes of his Church towards 'separated brethren' but is quick to see the need for penitence on the part of the mainline churches, fearless to point out the weaknesses of individualistic or separatist interpretations of the Spirit's work, wonderfully biblical, utterly open to God, and thrilled with the reality of the Lord the Spirit. The book glows with the Spirit's presence.

Here you will find much that you do not expect: God's surprises are emphasised. The baptism in the Holy Spirit is put in a wider framework than I have previously encountered. The link between Pentecost and the Parousia is dominant. The pivotal role of Israel is brought sharply into focus. And the book is firmly directed to the contemporary church. I believe it will be widely influential. It deserves to be.

Michael Green
Adviser in Evangelism to the
Archbishops of Canterbury and York

# INTRODUCTION

Like my previous book *One Lord One Spirit One Body*,[1] this new work is a reflection on the significance of a contemporary work of the Holy Spirit. Whereas the earlier work was limited to the charismatic movement, the present volume addresses together the significance of the Pentecostal and charismatic movements, which are presented as essentially one work of the Holy Spirit in different contexts. *One Lord One Spirit One Body* had more modest aims than the present work; it sought to examine the basic characteristics of the charismatic movement, to underline its essentially ecumenical character and then to offer some reflections and guidelines as to how to receive such an ecumenical grace into our divided Churches. It sought to provide an ecumenical methodology for all Christians caught up in this work of God so as to avoid the extremes of exclusive denominationalism on the one side and iconoclastic non-denominationalism on the other.

This new book is broader and more ambitious in scope. It is still focused on penetrating the significance of this contemporary work of the Holy Spirit. It directly addresses the mixed character of the Pentecostal and charismatic movements, both what is wonderfully from God and what is woefully from sinful humans; hence the title *The Glory and the Shame*. With each passing year this sharp contrast has become more evident, between the extraordinary vitality and impact of this work of God, and the debilitating trivialization and even appalling abuses that can so disfigure it.

*The Glory and the Shame* addresses in a fuller ecumenical framework the challenge to the Churches, and what
it means for whole Churches to be renewed in the Holy
Spirit. In particular, it gives more attention to the role
of Israel and the unexpected rise of Messianic Judaism.
It also highlights eschatology, bringing out the essential
link between Pentecost and Parousia.

The book seeks to draw out from the Scriptures guidelines and principles that are applicable to all Christian
Churches and traditions. Part II in particular begins with
the Scriptures and then applies the biblical principles to
the contemporary movement. Every fresh coming of the
Spirit inevitably challenges all those to whom it comes,
and so the ecumenical grace of baptism in the Spirit
challenges every Christian Church. The coming of the
Spirit always confirms what in each tradition is of the
Spirit of God and convicts of that which is not of the Spirit
(see John 16:7–15). The force of the challenge is as great to
each Church and tradition as to any other, because in all
Churches the gold of the Spirit becomes mixed with the
dross of the world. What is of the Spirit in each tradition
has an intensive and an extensive aspect: intensive as to
what is being currently lived by the power of the Spirit,
extensive as to the elements of church life that originate
from the Spirit's gift. As a convinced Roman Catholic,
the author believes that the elements coming from the
Spirit are more extensive in the ancient Churches of
East and West. However, as a Christian graced with the
friendship of many in other Christian Churches, he has
also to recognize that Christians not in communion with
Rome can have a clearer grasp on some key elements of
the gospel, and they may be living more intensively from
what quantitatively is a lesser patrimony.

With the Catholic and Orthodox Churches, there is
more to be challenged and sifted: more to be confirmed
as the work of the Spirit and more to be purged through
repentance. This is because the traditions of the Catholic and Orthodox Churches have 'more': more doctrine,
more liturgy, more theology, more history, more diversity.
Subjectively, however, the challenge is as great to all,

because all must allow the Spirit to sift what is most dear to them. The sifting has both a painful and a joyful side, for it is the word of the cross cutting through the mixture of spirit and of flesh; it is the pain of pruning that leads to the joy of more fruit from the vine.

The Orthodox Churches are deliberately mentioned in this introduction, as an acknowledgment of their importance in the whole *oikoumene*, since there is little reference to them in the main text. This omission reflects the virtual absence of an identifiable movement of charismatic renewal in the Orthodox world, though it is clear that there are various currents of spiritual renewal in the Orthodox Churches, including some with charismatic manifestations. The reasons for the distinctiveness of Orthodox patterns and attitudes in this area are complex, but would include: the long tradition of charismatic-type phenomena among the Orthodox; Orthodox pride in the Eastern emphasis on the Holy Spirit by comparison to Western neglect; the totally liturgical character of Orthodox piety; the lack of freedom of the faithful in the many Orthodox Churches in lands dominated by Islam or until recently by Communism; vigorous opposition to distinct charismatic renewal in some Orthodox Churches in the Western world, which see it as a product of Western and particularly American individualism.

The formulation of a common methodology of renewal for all Churches is not a rejection of the particularities of the different confessions. Nor is it a democratic levelling, as though every Church or Christian grouping, old or new, is the same kind of entity. It is simply asserting that we can find in the Scriptures principles applicable to all, because we are all the children of the one Father, redeemed by the one Saviour, and born of the one Spirit. The common grace of baptism in the Spirit highlights our common roots in the divine Trinity, and requires the formulation of a common methodology to bring forth the fruits of this gift for renewal and unity. Without a common methodology, this astonishing ecumenical grace is in danger of dissipation and this graced hour of becoming a tragically wasted opportunity.

I owe a great debt of gratitude to my brothers and sisters in the Mother of God Community. The Community has sought over the past twenty-five years to probe more deeply the foundational grace of baptism in the Spirit and to make this the basis for a corporate life under the guidance of the Spirit. It is only because I have been part of this experience in corporate renewal that I have been able to penetrate the fuller work of God in this way. A book such as this would have been quite impossible had I been a lone scholar grappling with a maze of data, but without the fellowship of the Spirit.

Finally, I should explain that the words 'Church', 'Pentecostal' and others are sometimes used with a capital letter and sometimes without. 'Church' with the capital refers to particular ecclesial traditions or denominations, while 'church' without the capital refers to local assemblies. 'Pentecostal' with the capital pertains to the denominations known by that name, while 'pentecostal' without a capital pertains to the grace and event of Pentecost.

Peter Hocken
June 1993

# Part I

## Outpouring

# CHAPTER ONE

# A SIGN OF CONTRADICTION

## An Astonishing Mixture

A cursory examination of the Pentecostal–charismatic phenomenon demonstrates both its explosive power and its complexity. Although segments of the movement may be in decline, worldwide the phenomenon continues to mushroom and multiply. But wherever it appears, the signs are mixed, the signals confused. Leaders of manifest integrity and holiness of life are matched by religious entrepreneurs of less obvious quality, who in some cases fall into grave sin, not only in the United States.

A power has been let loose: remarkable conversions and healings occur; new patterns of ministry emerge; gifts of the Spirit long regarded as rare or unavailable become regular features of congregational life; new forms of sharing between Catholic and Protestant, unthinkable in past generations, have sprung up. But honesty requires the recognition that these wonderful signs of God's powerful presence often have an underside that is less admirable. All is not glory and light.

It is important to reflect with open hearts and critical discernment upon this extraordinary phenomenon. Simply to be critical is to risk missing the glory and the grace; but to be enthusiastic without discernment risks welcoming the viruses that obscure the glory and sully the grace.

## Signs of the Creativity of the Holy Spirit

The Pentecostal and charismatic movements have given birth to waves of praise and worship throughout the

Church. Hearts are kindled, tongues are loosed, limbs are set free, so that the whole human person and whole congregations of the faithful can be immersed in the worship and praise of the Triune God by the power of the indwelling Spirit. New songs of praise spring up wherever the Spirit blows. This is always a characteristic of the unleashing of the Holy Spirit: the hearts, minds and faculties of Christians are set free and energized in creative worship and service of the Creator and Redeemer. Yet even here all is not wonder and grace; there can be emotional indulgence, enjoyment of the good feelings of exuberant worship more than love of the heavenly Lord; new songs can be trivial and lack doctrinal substance; worship can degenerate into stale repetition of our twenty favourite choruses. Signs of a wonderful gift, yes; but indications of human frailty too.

New forms of community life illustrate the Spirit's power in reconciliation: between separated Christians, between the haves and the have-nots, between white, brown and black. Here, a charismatic community gives an astonishing witness of love for the most deprived, and the power of God in reconciliation between races, and social classes. There, another community integrates Catholics and Protestants in a way that shatters the stereotypes of centuries. But even as we are admiring the Spirit's power to reconcile in divine love, we are confronted by division, by further schisms and secessions among those appealing to the Holy Spirit.

These movements have given rise to new forms of community life and of deeper Christian dedication. Perhaps the biggest explosion has taken place in France, where certainly it is the best documented. Less known but equally remarkable is the flourishing of new communities in the Far East, especially Malaysia and the Philippines. This surge seems impossible to explain apart from the leading of the Holy Spirit: seeing the number of remarkable conversions, the love of prayer and adoration, the thrust to evangelization, the witness of simplicity of life and identification with the poor and suffering. However, other communities that began with a flourish and great

hopes did not survive: Grenoble in France; and Chula
Vista, Erie and Houston in the U.S. have sadder tales
to tell. Rather unusually, the ups and downs of the
largely Mennonite Reba Place Fellowship in Evanston,
Illinois, are told with refreshing honesty by Dave and
Neta Jackson.[1] Other prominent communities with major
influence have hit hard times and have experienced tensions, divisions and a struggle for survival.

These movements of the Spirit have led to an intensified expectation of Jesus' return in glory. Given the
prominence of this eschatological hope in the New Testament, we can see here another sign of the Spirit's
presence. The prayer 'Come, Lord Jesus' can only rise
from hearts truly touched and convicted by the Holy
Spirit. But in this too we find ambiguity and even scandal. The same movements that rejoice in an intensified
expectation of the Lord's return have also given rise to a
plethora of naive and bizarre scenarios for the last days,
even in the more extreme instances to predictions of the
actual date.

The Pentecostal and charismatic movements have produced men and women of outstanding dedication and
holiness. From the outpouring of the Spirit at Azusa
Street in 1906, many heroic souls volunteered for missionary service. The work of the American Lillian Trasher
in Egypt; of the Chawners from Canada, father and son,
in Mozambique; of Englishman Willie Burton in Zaire
were matched by many lesser-known pioneers in jungle
and desert. The Bradford plumber Smith Wigglesworth
was a man of heroic stature, a giant of faith by anyone's
standards. Seemingly the charismatic movement has
not been characterized by as many figures of heroic
proportions, maybe because it was less despised. Nonetheless, the link between the Spirit of power and the
Spirit of holiness has been manifested in many lives:
in the dedication of courageous evangelists, in the pastor who moved from West Germany to the East in
obedience to the Lord, in the courageous witness of
Eastern European leaders, who kept a flame of faith
burning in the midst of drabness and suppression; in

the life of David Watson of whom his former Archbishop, Lord Blanch, said: 'David was a burning and shining light for the Church, and for the Church of England in particular, which he loved.'[2] Another saintly figure who commanded immense respect was Thomas Roberts, the Welsh missionary to France who refused to leave his adopted country in the years of Nazi occupation and who became an apostle of reconciliation between all Christians.

Nonetheless here too we have to recognize that it is not always obvious that the charismatic renewal produces holiness of life. Many a sympathetic observer has been troubled by the self-absorption of some charismatic groups, apparently seeking personal gratification more than the glory of God and deliverance from sin. The amazing gifts and phenomena that come with charismatic renewal can be trivialized and distorted in the service of self-aggrandizement and self-advertisement.

Even the extraordinary statistics may fail to impress, because of the suspicion of exaggeration, distortion and manipulation. The atmosphere of triumphalism that can characterize Pentecostal and charismatic circles is very off-putting to humble and sensitive Christians. Christian life can be presented as an uninterrupted succession of miracles, prophetic messages and victories over Satan, accompanied by constant expansion and evangelistic success. As a result many claims made for the movement are sceptically received. Fortunately, one person convinced of the major significance of this current is the world's foremost Christian statistician, David B. Barrett, an Anglican priest working for the U.S. Southern Baptist Foreign Mission Board, who is a sympathetic observer. Barrett, who has produced some astonishing statistics, writes:

The sheer magnitude and diversity of the numbers involved beggar the imagination ... The Pentecostals, charismatics, and third-wavers who make up this Renewal today number 21 per cent of organized global Christianity ... One quarter of the world's full-time Christian workers are Pentecostals/ charismatics.[3]

## Reflection

This combination of data, what we may call the glory and the shame, points to one conclusion: that this movement is of the Spirit, but is much mixed with the flesh. Holding the most brilliant promise, it may easily not fulfil that hope. A most precious gift, its present condition remains fragile.

Without the powerful presence of the Holy Spirit at the outset, there would have been no Pentecostal movement, no charismatic renewal and no charisms. Without the Spirit, there would have been no upsurge of praise and worship, no wave of new communities, no flame of evangelism, no intensified longing for the second coming nor any other evident fruits of this renewal. But the fruit of this outpouring is clearly not automatic, never a foregone conclusion. There is a gift to be received, a call to be obeyed, a task to be fulfilled, a battle to be won.

The Pentecostal–charismatic movement is not simply a success story. It is a wonderful and undeserved grace, that charismatic believers may yet squander and the Churches tolerate rather than welcome, or worse still, ignore or oppose. This book is written in the hope that more Christians may grasp the vastness of the issues at stake and help to avert the dreadful tragedy that its evaporation would represent.

# CHAPTER TWO

# THE SURPRISES OF THE HOLY SPIRIT

Any sovereign outpouring of divine blessing is necessarily unexpected, for the invasion of the Spirit is never predictable. There is always in such theophanies an element of surprise: surprise as to location, surprise as to timing and surprise as to content. Even in revivals repeating patterns of past outpourings, the visible power of the Spirit to convict and transform never conforms to a set stereotype.

## A Series of Surprises

The unfolding of the Pentecostal–charismatic movement of the twentieth century has been marked by a series of major surprises, that we may call the surprises of the Holy Spirit. The focus on surprise is not a concentration on extraordinary phenomena, but a reflection on the unexpectedness of these interventions of God. Surprises result from the disparity between the greatness of the divine work and the limitations of human understanding. God's works surprise us because they do not conform to our expectations and do not fit into our received categories. Attention to the surprises is important because they show where we need to revise our thinking and expand our categories to the scope of God's acts.

The first surprise is the *Pentecostal movement*. This surprise is not just people speaking in other tongues. The Spirit of God was poured out in a way that gave rise to an identifiable move of God's power across the world.

This 'Pentecost' had characteristic signs that appeared wherever it occurred. The manner of its appearance was also remarkable; nobody would expect a major move of the Spirit to break out at an inter-racial meeting led by a black pastor in a poor area of Los Angeles in the midst of rather fringe Holiness groups. The reaction of many was to ask whether anything good could come out of California, echoing Nathanael's opinion of Nazareth (John 1:46).

The surprise is not just the *who* but also the *what*: what happened to people at Azusa Street and what they did were just as astonishing as the setting and the company. People spoke in unknown tongues, they prophesied, they raised their voices in simultaneous praise, and some were healed. They spoke of experiencing 'Pentecost' and of being baptized in the Holy Spirit.

For various reasons the mainline Churches were not ready to recognize the presence of the Holy Spirit in such phenomena. In North America the established Protestant Churches had little sympathy for frontier revivalism. Some within the Holiness stream denounced it as devilish and demonic, a position bluntly expressed in the Berlin Declaration of German Holiness leaders in 1909, which characterized the movement as 'nicht von oben, sondern von unten' (not from on high, but from below). In Britain, the Evangelical Holiness conventions at Keswick represented the main point of rejection. In general, the Pentecostals were dismissed as fanatical 'holy rollers', a fringe phenomenon of no interest to serious and sober Christians.

The second surprise was the beginning of *charismatic renewal in the historic Protestant traditions*. Though without any one centre of outbreak like Azusa Street, circles of Christians in the mainline Protestant Churches experienced over several years the same pattern of blessing as the Pentecostals. In April 1960, Dennis Bennett, an Episcopal priest, told his Californian congregation of the spiritual odyssey that had led to his speaking in tongues. Subsequent publicity spread the news of this new move of the Spirit among mainline Protestants. Other centres of neo-Pentecostal blessing became known over the next few years; in particular the Presbyterian Church of James Brown (Parkesburg, Pennsylvania), the Dutch Reformed Church of Harald Bredesen (Mount Vernon, New York) and the Lutheran Church of Larry Christenson (San Pedro, California). In Britain, pioneer figures included Michael Harper (Anglican) and Charles Clarke (Methodist); in the Netherlands, Wim Verhoef (Reformed); in Germany, Arnold Bittlinger (Lutheran).

Though the Pentecostal movement had been spreading throughout the world for half a century, this irruption of pentecostal phenomena in the midst of traditional Protestantism was no less disturbing. Press coverage mostly focused on tongues, beginning with *Newsweek* and *Time* in 1960. A 1964 article in the *Saturday Evening Post* of New York City reported: 'The name glossolalia sounds as strange as the act itself. But this practice of praying in "unknown tongues" spreads, and brings prophecies of still stranger things to come.'

This development among mainline Protestants did not correspond at all to Pentecostal expectations. The Pentecostals regarded the mainline Churches as dead and beyond resuscitation. This was why the Holy Spirit had raised them up. It was the distinctive ministry of Pentecostal David du Plessis, foretold in a prophecy by Smith Wigglesworth in 1936, to witness to the authenticity of this 'new move', which he and his friend Donald Gee were to call 'Pentecost outside Pentecost'. Both du Plessis and Gee played an important role in helping Pentecostals to overcome these suspicions.

Neither did this second surprise correspond at all to what any Protestant Churches expected or where they looked for renewal. Church leaders and theologians among Lutherans and Southern Baptists, for example, had quite different attitudes to the need for renewal in the first place; neither they nor any other Church establishments expected anything positive from the Pentecostals, who were perceived as fanatical and uneducated, typified by emotional excess and by naive literalism in their reading of the Bible.

The third surprise was the spread of *charismatic renewal to the Roman Catholic Church*. In retrospect, it may seem natural that the spread of charismatic renewal to the mainline Protestant Churches should be followed by the penetration of Roman Catholicism. However, that was not the perspective of the early 1960s. The gulf between Rome and the Reform meant that neither side expected spiritual renewal to spring up on the far bank, let alone cross this historic divide. It was particularly shocking for the Pentecostals and for staunch charismatic Evangelicals, who were still a rare species in 1967. For Pentecostals, only recently coming to terms with the idea of baptized-in-the-Spirit Christians in historic Protestant Churches, the Roman extension was mostly experienced as a sharp jolt, rekindling their doubts about 'Pentecost outside Pentecost'. Most assumed that it was impossible for the Lord to revive the Church of Rome, and could only accommodate the idea of charismatic Catholics on the supposition that they would soon leave their apostate Church and join the Pentecostal ranks.

The appearance of 'Catholic Pentecostalism', as it was first designated, did not of course correspond at all to what Catholics expected. In the late 1960s, renewal was high on the Catholic agenda, as the goal of the recently-concluded Second Vatican Council. But attention was fixed on liturgical reform, renewal of biblical studies, rethinking of catechetical practice, promoting lay participation, etc. No Catholic imagined that the renewal of Catholic life would or could come from the restoration of the *charismata pneumatika* of 1 Corinthians 12, especially when their source was perceived as narrowly sectarian. It is true that Cardinal Suenens had made a speech at the Council about charisms, which had led to a positive and optimistic paragraph in the Constitution on the Church (para. 12). But the Cardinal and the Council fathers were hardly aware of the additional relevance this paragraph would acquire three years later when these spiritual gifts actually broke out among lay Catholics in the United States.

The fourth surprise was the rise of *Messianic Judaism*,

the first time a distinctively Jewish form of Christianity has emerged since the early centuries of the Church. Most Evangelicals and Pentecostals were already convinced that Israel would accept Jesus as the Messiah in the end times in accordance with Romans 11:25–26. However, they were not anticipating a truly Jewish form of Christianity, only Jewish conversions to Gentile Christianity on a bigger scale. Conversions among Jews have been increasing, not simply through more effective Gentile evangelism, but often through sovereign acts of God's grace towards Jews. As a result, Jews accepting Jesus (Yeshua) as the Messiah have sought to affirm their ongoing Jewish identity, as 'completed' or 'fulfilled' Jews. Largely through this charismatic impulse, Christian or Messianic synagogues have been springing up, celebrating Jewish feasts and developing distinctively Jewish patterns of worship (including music and dance), all in a framework confessing Jesus as Messiah. Their preferred designation as 'Messianic Jews' enables them to identify with Jesus as Jewish Messiah, without any connotation of abandoning their Jewish heritage for what in Jewish eyes is the historically suspect religion of 'Christianity'.

Messianic Judaism was a total surprise, even though there were a few prophetic Jewish Christians who had longed and prayed for such a development. While Evangelicals have always targeted Jews for evangelistic campaigns, many Catholics and other Christians involved in ecumenical dialogue had been moving away from all idea of evangelization of the people of the old covenant. As a result, many Christians today are unaware of the rise of Messianic Judaism; among those who have heard, it is often a taboo topic, an embarrassment that threatens the progress of Christian–Jewish dialogue.

## Non-Denominational Charismatics

This schema of four surprises in an expanding circle of pentecostal blessing does not however account for the whole charismatic phenomenon.[1] To these four groupings must be added one that does not fit into the sequence: that is the highly complex scene of independent or 'non-denominational' charismatic groups and ministries – in British parlance the 'House Churches'. The surprise element here is not that independency of this kind should arise but lies in the rapidity of its growth and its emergence as a major new sector in the overall movement. Thus in one way it is a fifth surprise, but the surprise element is less than in the other four instances.

Because the non-denominationals represent a major new development, this topic needs more extended study. It is not an evasion of their significance and challenge to defer that reflection to later chapters. The focus here is not only on the surprises listed, but on their sequence and its meaning. This meaning is not lessened by the existence of a stream that does not immediately fit into the pattern.

## Surprise and Challenge

Each surprise represents a profound challenge to inherited ways of thinking. Each surprise after the first represents the same work of the Holy Spirit spreading to a different context. Since each surprise bears the marks of the Holy Spirit, it is important that we allow ourselves to be challenged to the full. The challenge is ultimately that God does not act according to our theories and our presuppositions. God is bigger than our categories. 'How great are thy works, O Lord! Thy thoughts are very deep!' (Ps 92:5).

It is natural to seek to fit new impressions into existing frameworks of understanding. Surprises challenge these received frameworks. The temptation is to make one of two mistakes:

(1) either to ignore the inconvenient facts and continue with basically unchanged theories, or

(2) to make minor modifications that appear to respond to the new events, but really not face up to the extent of the challenge.

In this situation it is important not to seek some quick explanation, but to weigh seriously the new evidence against our exegetical, theological and ecclesial convictions. Surprises of the Lord never contradict the age-long work of God. But they will challenge the ways our understandings have deviated from the heart of the gospel and the fulness of the mystery of Christ. In the interaction between the data of God's surprises and our received understanding, the Spirit of God will work a purification and deepening that will build on all that has been the work of the Spirit in past ages while opening us up to unsuspected treasures.

Taking all the data seriously suggests at the least that:

(1)  all the Churches have a significance in God's plan;

(2)  the reappearance of Jewish Christianity is an essential component in this work of God;

(3)  the non-denominational groupings also belong to the over-all pattern;

(4)  the Pentecostal movement was the mother of these surprises;

(5)  baptism in the Spirit is the common grace.

In other words, our explanations and presentations of this total phenomenon have to do justice to all these factors, if they are to do justice to the extraordinary scope of God's work.

# CHAPTER THREE

# A COMPARISON WITH THE ACTS OF THE APOSTLES

It is not really possible to understand contemporary events without seeking for historical parallels. The rise of the Pentecostal–charismatic current of life in the twentieth century requires that we look for any historical parallels, and see whether there are any precedents for the series of surprises of the Spirit examined in the last chapter.

The key question is this: Have there been any other series of divine interventions in which two conditions are fulfilled: (a) that the series involves recognizably the same blessing being poured out on quite different groups of people; and (b) that each subsequent new milieu represents a wholly unexpected grace of the Lord for those believed to be beyond the scope of such a blessing?

The Protestant world has seen a number of revivals which bear the marks of being 'heaven-sent'; that is 'prayed down' rather than 'worked up'; for example, the Welsh Revivals of 1859 and 1904, the East African revival dating from the 1930s and the more localized Lewis revival of 1949 in the Outer Hebrides. But while manifesting the evident signs of the Spirit's work, conviction of sin and conversion of heart, reverence for the blood of Jesus and worship of the Saviour, these revivals did not break the boundaries of the worlds in which they occurred.

There are also in Christian history several examples of spiritual influences spreading from one milieu to another, including some surprising crossing of Church barriers. Thus, writings of the French Catholics, Archbishop François Fénelon and Madame Jeanne Guyon on the interior life were welcomed, albeit with occasional editing, among American Holiness circles of the nineteenth century. Another would be the remarkable diffusion throughout the late twelfth century and early thirteenth century Europe of the ideal of evangelical simplicity and poverty in imitation of the apostolic pattern described in the gospel missions. But these are instances of the spread of inspiring ideas and teaching, rather than the unexpected occurrence of a recognizably identical grace-experience.

The one instance of such a series in Christian history, that is demonstrably parallel to the series of surprises of the Spirit in the Pentecostal and charismatic movements, is that found in the Acts of the Apostles. Here too each surprise in the sequence represents both a recognizably identical work of the Holy Spirit, and its extension to new milieux, unimaginable to the earlier recipients.

## The Series of Surprises in the Book of Acts

In the account of Acts, the first surprise is the *event of Pentecost*. Even though the prophets had promised the gift of the Spirit, and of a new heart, even though Jesus had told them to wait in the city 'until you are clothed with power from on high' (Luke 24:49), what happened to the disciples was overwhelming and unimaginable. It has so many dimensions: theophany ('the rush of a mighty wind [that] filled all the house'); corporate ('devout men from every nation under heaven'); praise of God ('telling the mighty works of God'); speaking in other languages; prophecy.

The outpouring of the Spirit at Pentecost was, however, restricted to those who were fully submitted to the Law of Moses, both 'Jews and proselytes' (Acts 2:10).[1] The proselytes were full Gentile converts to Judaism, who accepted circumcision and all the obligations of the Law.

The second surprise is not the outpouring on Cornelius, but the *conversion of the Samaritans*. The risen Jesus had said to the apostles: 'You shall be my witnesses in Jerusalem and in all Judea and Samaria and to the end of the earth' (Acts 1:8). How was the gospel to be brought to Samaria? The attitude of the Jews to the Samaritans was little different from pre-ecumenical Catholic and Protestant attitudes to each other. There was total disdain and non-communication; 'for Jews have no dealings with Samaritans' (John 4:9). The Jews of Jesus' day could not imagine a Jew preaching to the Samaritans, much less that the Samaritans could receive the same grace of God as themselves.

This happened first due to persecution; Christians, especially the Greek-speakers, had to leave Jerusalem. Secondly, it was due to the boldness and obedience of Philip, later called an evangelist (Acts 21:8) and depicted as a man particularly attentive to the initiatives of the Spirit (Acts 8:26–27, 39–40). An obedience to the Spirit similar to his pursuit of the Ethiopian eunuch (see Acts 8:26–27) may have been behind Philip's earlier visit: 'Philip went down to a city of Samaria, and proclaimed to them the Christ' (Acts 8:5). This obedience of Philip required a remarkable inner abandonment of Jewish mentalities concerning the Samaritans.

The decision of the apostles to send Peter and John to Samaria was itself a response to a surprise of the Spirit. They must have sensed that the opening up of the gospel to the Samaritans was something momentous, that required the support and ratification of the Twelve. The narrative records: 'Then they laid their hands on them and they received the Holy Spirit' (Acts 8:17). That is to say, the Samaritans received the same gift of God as the Jewish Christians (cf 8:17 with 2:38).

Why are the Samaritans mentioned before Cornelius the God-fearer? Probably because the Samaritans practised circumcision, whereas the God-fearers though welcome at the synagogue were not circumcised.

Before recording the conversion of Cornelius, Luke moves from Samaria to the story of the Ethiopian eunuch. The eunuch appears to be a God-fearer, that is a Gentile, who worshipped the God of Israel without having been circumcised and without accepting all the requirements of the Law. In this case, he was in the same situation as Cornelius. Maybe Luke tells the story of the eunuch in Acts 8, as further evidence of the charismatic activity of Philip, opening out now to a Gentile – who is baptized not circumcised – but where the transient contact did not challenge the Church to the same degree as the events in Caesarea.

We come now to the third surprise, *the falling of the Spirit upon Cornelius and his household*. The Christian baptism of a God-fearer would not have posed great problems, as long as the Gentile convert still retained a second-level associate status, since only the circumcised were recognized as fully part of Israel. But this is precisely what the vision of Peter made clear: the separation based on the Law was at an end. The clinching argument for Peter is that the blessing given to the Gentiles is identical to that of the Jewish Christians on the Day of Pentecost:

> As I began to speak, the Holy Spirit fell on them *just as on us at the beginning*. And I remembered the word of the Lord, how he said, 'John baptized with water, but you shall be baptized with the Holy Spirit.' If then God gave *the same gift to them as he gave to us* when we believed in the Lord Jesus Christ, who was I that I could withstand God? (Acts 11:15–17; italics mine)

There is a conflict between the apostles' received theology and the visible work of the Holy Spirit. Their theology said: Israel is the chosen people; entry to Israel is through circumcision; status with God is based on circumcision and observance of the Law. The evidence said: these Gentiles have received the identical gift of the Spirit. Peter's appeal is twofold: to the prophecy of the Lord, and to the evidence of the Spirit, that they all manifested the same signs; speaking with tongues, proclaiming the praises of the Lord.

This series of surprises reaches its full course with the

*conversion of Gentiles in Antioch*, who had not previously accepted the God of Israel. 'But there were some of them, men of Cyprus and Cyrene, who on coming to Antioch spoke to the Greeks also, preaching the Lord Jesus. And the hand of the Lord was with them, and a great number that believed turned to the Lord' (Acts 11:20–21).

## Reflection

We can now consider the similarities and the dissimilarities between the surprises of the Holy Spirit in the first century and in the twentieth:

## Similarities

(1) There is a direct parallel as to the character of the events. In each case, there is an outpouring of the Holy Spirit of God, touching the core of people's lives. Both recall the prophecy that Jesus will baptize with the Holy Spirit. Both involve manifestation of the gifts of the Spirit. In both cases, the outpoured Spirit leads to evangelistic power and dramatic impact. These points confirm the fundamental validity and appropriateness of the comparison.

(2) What happens in both series is more than the actualization of current religious expectations and longings. The events have a transcendent character. The surprise is not just that the people were not expecting this at that time, but that what happened was beyond their imagining.

(3) Acceptance of the divine event (and the breadth of God's working) is by believing the word of prophecy and accepting the evidence of the Spirit before their eyes. The objective signs of the Spirit's working are the same. Acceptance of this evidence requires a radical expansion in their theology.

(4) In both series, each new phase builds on those that have gone before. God's purpose is unfolding through the series of surprises. Both sequences are quite different from 'new waves' which take the place of previous waves now seen as exhausted or no longer operative.

(5) It would appear that the twentieth-century developments are in some way the inverse of those of the first century. In the first century the movement was outward from Jews and proselytes, through Samaritans and God-fearers to complete pagans. This sequence in the Acts of the Apostles has an obvious meaning, expressed by Luke in Acts 1:8, of the gospel being taken out by steps from the Jews towards 'the ends of the earth'. The twentieth-century sequence begins from the fringe of institutional historic Christianity and works back towards the old and the venerable (historic Protestant Churches, the Roman Catholic Church, Judaism).

## Dissimilarities

(1) The first-century movement concerns the spread of Christianity itself, while the twentieth century represents the spread of a particular pattern of revival and renewal. This point does not invalidate the comparison, which depends on the nature of what is happening, but it may qualify some of the conclusions.

(2) The first series within a united Christianity contrasts with the second series occurring amidst considerable division. As a result, there is no overall framework for pastoral supervision of the second. Catholics believe the Lord has given a petrine ministry of service to the whole Church, but the papacy has itself become a major point of division between the Churches, as Paul VI lamented. This structural lack is a major factor in its vulnerability.

## Conclusion

The similarities are sufficiently striking for the comparison to have a general validity. The fundamental parallel lies in the occurrence of a Pentecost event, an outpouring of the Holy Spirit in a divinely-ordered sequence that opens up the divine promise to groupings far beyond the circle of the first recipients. The surprises lie both in the nature of the initial event and in each step of subsequent expansion.

This general validity can legitimately ground questions concerning the significance of the inverse order of recipients. If the overall comparison is valid, the twentieth-century sequence represents the pulling together of splintered Christianity including the healing of the prototypical breach between Jew and Gentile. While the inverse order suggests that the second series heralds the end of the Church era, it would be foolish to talk in terms of years or even decades or to make detailed chronological comparisons.

# CHAPTER FOUR

# THE WISDOM OF GOD

God is all-wise. Everything that proceeds from the hand of God expresses God's wisdom. God's sovereign interventions in the world and in the Church are necessarily an embodiment of divine wisdom. This pattern of sovereign intervention is supremely shown in the Incarnation when God's 'all-powerful word leaped from heaven, from the royal throne' (Wis 18:15) and took on human flesh.

It is worth reflecting on how God's wisdom may have been manifested in the origins of the Pentecostal and charismatic movements. The focus is on the origins because in sovereign moves of the Spirit the origins most clearly reveal the purpose of the Lord. This does not remove such movements from historical scrutiny, because every sovereign intervention of the Spirit is a leaping into history, so that the grace given becomes embodied and acquires a history.

In examining Pentecostal and charismatic origins for signs of God's wisdom, we need to retain a sense of proportion. Our knowledge is partial and imperfect. When we make confident judgments about why God did this and not that, we risk looking foolish. But it is still valuable to reflect prayerfully on our experience of God's initiatives, and humbly recognize what we can see of the divine wisdom, the divine love and the divine mercy. At the very least, we will see that it does not make sense to acknowledge these movements as a work of the Holy Spirit, and then to wish that they had begun in a different way; to think that it would have been better if they had begun in a less haphazard manner, e.g. in one identifiable place or in one specific Church.

## Pentecostal Origins

Many questions can be asked about Pentecostal origins. Historical research shows that Azusa Street was the primary catalyst for the worldwide Pentecostal movement, though not all Pentecostal impulses can be traced back to Los Angeles. For example, a strand not tributary to Azusa Street flowed from Zion City, Illinois; there were also other remarkable outbreaks like that at Mukti near Poona, India in the homes of child widows run by Pandita Ramabai.

Many regard the events at Topeka, Kansas at New Year 1901 under Charles Parham as the beginning of the Pentecostal movement. While Parham certainly had a preparatory role in the developments leading up to Azusa Street, there was nothing in the immediate aftermath of January 1901 to suggest an infectious outpouring of the Holy Spirit that would impact the world; the first tongues-speaker became silent about the event until after Azusa Street, few others were won over to the experience, and immediately after the Topeka events divine healing seems to have become the focus of Parham's preaching more than baptism in the Spirit.

Why Azusa Street, Los Angeles, California? Various features stand out: its inter-racial character, the make-up of the crowds who came from far and near, its fringe character in relation both to society and to the mainline denominations.

The inter-racial component at Azusa Street astounded all participants. This was surely an expression of divine wisdom, that such a worldwide explosion of grace should be unleashed at a gathering of the poor and dispossessed of all colours, led by an uneducated black pastor. These origins clearly express the divine gratuitousness, and the difference between God's plans and mere human ideas:

But God chose what is foolish in the world to shame the wise, God chose what is weak in the world

> to shame the strong, God chose what is low and
> despised in the world, even things that are not, to
> bring to nothing things that are, so that no human
> being might boast in the presence of God. (1 Cor.
> 1:27–29)

Recognizing divine purpose in the inter-racial character
of Pentecostal origins means seeing human sin and
tragedy in the subsequent loss of this dimension. The
re-establishment of the colour line in most Pentecostal
groups is a frightening reminder of the capacity of human
sin to disfigure the work of God. This loss is shameful. The
failure to acknowledge this sin in Pentecostal histories,
which generally breathe a somewhat triumphalist air, is
a serious blemish awaiting correction.

Why outside the mainline Churches? Firstly and para-
doxically, there may be an ecumenical reason in this
revival beginning 'outside'. A Los Angeles Methodist said
of Azusa Street in 1906: 'We wanted it to start in the First
Methodist Church, but God did not start it there. I bless
God that it did not start in any church in this city, but in
a barn, so that we might all come and take part in it.'

Secondly, the preparatory climate of ideas and expectations had developed mainly in the Holiness movement, which was being steadily eased out of American
Methodism in the last decades of the nineteenth century.
Several new Holiness groups had sprung up in the years
prior to Azusa Street, and the first battles provoked by
the Pentecostal revival were mostly controversies within
the Holiness movement. Since the terminology of baptism
in the Spirit was already current in Holiness circles, one
of the first conflicts concerned the nature of this baptism
and the evidence for its reception. Thus it was easy for
mainline Protestant Christians in North America to see
the Azusa revival, if they even heard of it, as another
fanatical variation in a movement already perceived as
a fringe phenomenon.

The European origins throw a different light on the relationship of the Pentecostal movement to the major Protestant Churches. In its first decade there were four major

leaders in Europe: the Methodist minister of English origin, Thomas Ball Barratt in Oslo, Norway; the Anglican priest Alexander Boddy at Monkwearmouth, Sunderland in north-eastern England; the Lutheran pastor Jonathan Paul at Berlin in Germany; and the ex-Salvation Army and Dowieite Gerrit Polman in Amsterdam, Holland. Barratt and Paul were nationally-known and respected ministers in their denominations; Boddy a convinced Anglican, though not well-known in his Church. Polman alone was without denominational convictions and commitments.

These origins suggest that the Pentecostal movement in Europe had at least a potential to become a trans-Church revival rather than an inevitable instrument of secession into new denominations. The reasons why this new movement did not significantly penetrate the Churches of these pioneer figures are complex, but a major factor was its rejection in Holiness circles, particularly the Keswick movement in Britain and the *Gemeinschaftsbewegung* in Germany. While Boddy failed to draw many Anglicans to Sunderland, Paul had more success in the state Protestant Church in Germany, but this was offset by the fiercely anti-Pentecostal Berlin Declaration of 1909.

So the question may be better phrased: why did the Pentecostal movement develop outside the old Churches and become a new family of denominations? Does this express divine wisdom, human weakness or both? For Christians from the historic traditions of East and West this is a challenging question.

From the derisive responses of mainline Protestants as they became aware of the Pentecostal revival, it would seem that there was no realistic hope of such a radical grace being given space to grow within their Churches at that time.[1] We can perhaps sense a divine wisdom in the Lord permitting this rejection so that the Pentecostal life in the Spirit, with the full range of charismata, could develop freely and find corporate expression in new settings. While Pentecostal independence exposed them to aberrations of doctrine and behaviour and their hostility to tradition led to forms of narrowness and one-sidedness, their freedom allowed them to develop the gifts and ministries of the Spirit in contexts unfettered by convention and unbelief. This freedom enabled the Pentecostals to develop a tradition of their own, not immune from the weaknesses of traditional frameworks, but able at a later date to enter into more positive relationships with the Churches that had initially spurned them.

## The First Stirrings of the Charismatic Movement

It is difficult to date the precise beginnings of the charismatic movement as the clear occurrence of 'Pentecost outside Pentecost'. When the term 'charismatic' was first used in this context (around 1963), it was distinguished from the Pentecostal movement by occurring within the mainline Churches. The subsequent explosion of non-denominational churches and ministries, arising from the grace of baptism in the Spirit but not identifying with the Pentecostals, led to the term 'charismatic movement' designating all 'Spirit-filled' bodies and people outside the classical Pentecostal movement.

There were many antecedents within the Protestant Churches to the public manifestation of the movement with the publicity surrounding Dennis Bennett. In the U.S.A. in the 1950s, there was the impact of the Full Gospel Business Men, reaching out beyond the Pentecostal Churches; there was the role of Agnes Sanford in circles devoted to divine healing, especially among Episcopalians; there was the impact on mainline Christians of the Pentecostal healing evangelists, especially Oral Roberts; there were ministers already baptized in the Spirit: the Presbyterian Jim Brown in Pennsylvania, the Episcopalian Richard Winkler in Wheaton, Illinois, and the more itinerant preachers, Harald Bredesen[2] and Tommy Tyson. Here and there we find reports of sovereign blessings upon a whole congregation, as with the Mennonite Gerald Derstine in Minnesota. The extent of this spread of pentecostal Christianity into the mainline Protestant Churches during the 1950s only became apparent after the news broke of Bennett's resignation from Van Nuys in 1960.

These beginnings represent a different pattern from the origins of the Pentecostal movement half a century earlier. Even more clearly than in the first decade of the century, there is no one founder figure. There is no equivalent to Azusa Street; no one place where 'it all happened'. While in time, particular churches became known as Spirit-filled beacons of light and blessing (like Jim Brown's in Pennsylvania and Dennis Bennett's in Seattle), none eclipsed the others in renown.

How might God's wisdom be reflected in this pattern? It is a story of slow but steady spread, initially largely unnoticed. It affected people in virtually all the Protestant denominations. Many were touched by the Lord through the ministry of Christians of traditions other than their own. The gradualness made it less threatening to the Churches, and reduced the danger of outright rejection. The simultaneous touching of many from different Churches was a clear sign that this grace does not belong to any one Church tradition or constituency. The Spirit is seen as being poured out upon *all flesh*, at least all Protestant flesh. The fact that something was going on for years before people became aware of it is also a humbling thought, reminding us that we are not the creators and givers of all meaning.

Mention has been made of the role and influence of Pentecostals in the charismatic origins. The data indicate: (a) Pentecostals were often God's instruments for bringing baptism in the Spirit to other Christians; and (b) they were far from being the only instruments. Many were led into charismatic experience from an interest in healing, others from their study of the Scriptures; some were touched by the Lord without any evident preparation. As we shall see, the role of David du Plessis was particularly significant in spreading this experience and in preserving the sense, sometimes rather tenuous, of the over-all unity and kinship of the Pentecostal and charismatic movements.

The charismatic movement was indebted to the Pentecostal movement in significant ways, but was not simply its offshoot. The evidence does suggest however that the charismatic renewal could not have happened in the way that it did without the prior rise of the Pentecostal movement. The grasp of baptism in the Spirit as its central grace was influenced by the Pentecostals and du Plessis in particular. Without them, it is possible that the movement would have had no clearer focus or shape than the vastly varied orders, missions and guilds promoting the ministry of divine healing.

## Catholic Charismatic Beginnings

Quite differently from the origins among Protestants, the charismatic movement among Roman Catholics began in a public manner that attracted immediate attention. The Catholic beginnings had several other facets that were distinctive:

- its corporate context
- its university setting
- the Church commitment of the pioneers
- the context of renewal associated with the Second Vatican Council.

All these features shaped the nascent charismatic renewal in the Roman Catholic Church. The friendship and co-operation existing among many in the original groups at the universities of Duquesne, Notre Dame and Michigan State led to the movement among Catholics having an initial coherence and identity that it had not known among the Protestants. The high degree of Church commitment and the post-conciliar context combined to give the Catholic movement a sense of mission to the Church that the Protestant currents had lacked. The previous experience of participants in Catholic renewal groups added a sense of strategy and a flair for organization.

It is not hard to detect signs of divine wisdom in these

beginnings of Catholic charismatic renewal. The combination of corporate character and Church commitment
shows, perhaps more clearly than anything else, that the
Holy Spirit is interested in renewing the Roman Catholic
Church. It is not the only sign of this intent, but it is one
well designed to overcome the scepticism of Pentecostals
and Evangelicals with deep-seated antipathies to 'Rome'.
Not one of the Catholics baptized in the Spirit in those
1967 beginnings believed that the Lord was calling them
out of the Roman Catholic Church.

The public beginnings of charismatic renewal among
Catholics contributed to its rapid spread. This may reflect
divine wisdom, for such beginnings in any Protestant
Church would probably have provoked more negative
reactions. That this did not happen in the Roman Catholic Church owed much to more flexible Church structures and the renewal context of the Second Vatican
Council. The timing of this remarkable event could be
called exquisite. The Catholic Church was in the thick
of implementing the renewal decrees of the Council,
touching virtually all areas of church life. The Catholic
commitment of these charismatic neophytes predisposed
them to see this Pentecost-event in terms of the Church
renewal promoted by the Second Vatican Council. They
interpreted the baptism in the Spirit as a realization of
the renewal sought by the Council; they saw a direct
connection between their experience and the initiatives
of Pope John XXIII in calling a Council and praying for a
'new Pentecost'. In other words, the Catholic beginnings
of early 1967 not only extended the boundaries of the
movement in a major way; they introduced a new vision
of Church renewal in an ecumenical setting.

## Messianic Judaism

The wisdom of the Lord in the rise of Messianic Judaism
may perhaps be most clearly sensed in its burgeoning
in the years following the six-day war of 1967, which
ended the centuries-long domination of Jerusalem by the
Gentiles. For this event appears to be a fulfilment of the
prophecy of Jesus in Luke 21:24.

In view of the suffering and persecution experienced by the Jews at the hands of Christians, it is very hard for Jews to give credibility to Gentile proclamations of Jesus. In the situation of the diaspora, for any Jew to accept Jesus as Messiah was to be separated from the Jewish heritage. The return of the Jews to the land has created a situation in which Jews can without suspicion of disloyalty take an interest in Jesus the prophet who has made their land known to the world. This is a first step towards Jews being able to accept Jesus without abandoning their Jewish heritage. The rise of Messianic Judaism begins to make this possible.

Messianic Jews do not ordinarily identify themselves as charismatics, much as they do not like to call themselves 'Christians' in view of the pejorative associations of this term in the eyes of the Jewish people. However, it is clear that Messianic Judaism is predominantly charismatic and that in the wisdom of God it required the massive energy of this outpouring of the Spirit to make possible the creative interaction of Jewish forms of worship with confession of Jesus as the Messiah. What is in effect a radically new liturgy, at once Jewish and Christian, could hardly have been produced by a church committee; it needed the infusion of life and power from on high.

# CHAPTER FIVE

# BAPTISM IN THE SPIRIT

The common factor in each surprise of the Holy Spirit in the Pentecostal and charismatic movements is the spiritual event generally called the baptism in the Holy Spirit. Any reflection on this modern phenomenon must give particular attention to the reality and meaning of baptism in the Spirit. Such a study has two poles: first, the relevant scriptural data and, secondly, the contemporary experience, especially the reasons why this foundational grace has been designated the baptism in the Holy Spirit.

## The Data from the New Testament

The New Testament contains six specific references to baptizing or being baptized with/in the Holy Spirit: Matt 3:11; Mark 1:8; Luke 3:16; John 1:33; Acts 1:5; 11:16.

(1) The declaration by John the Baptist found in all three synoptic gospels concerning 'he who is coming after me', contrasts John's baptizing with water to his successor's baptizing with Holy Spirit[1] (Matt 3:11; Mark 1:8; Luke 3:16). The Matthean and Lukan versions are longer: both add 'and fire' after the Holy Spirit, followed by a word concerning judgment and separation: 'His winnowing fork is in his hand, and he will clear his threshing floor and gather his wheat into the granary, but the chaff he will burn with unquenchable fire' (Matt 3:12; Luke 3:17).

(2) The fourth gospel links this baptismal role of

Jesus not only with his own reception but also with his ongoing possession of the Holy Spirit: 'He who sent me to baptize with water said to me, "He on whom you see the Spirit descend *and remain*, this is he who baptizes with the Holy Spirit' (John 1:33 italics mine).

(3)   Twice in the Acts of the Apostles, the contrast is made between the baptismal ministries of John and of Jesus, but the saying is attributed to the risen Jesus (1:5; 11:16). Jesus' baptismal role is here in the passive, 'you shall be baptized with Holy Spirit', leaving implicit the identity of the baptizer. These words are evidently understood by Luke as having a fulfilment on the day of Pentecost (see the 'before many days' in Acts 1:5) and in the events in the household of Cornelius at Caesarea described in Acts 10 (see Peter's recalling this 'word of the Lord' in Acts 11:16).

There are no other references to the Baptist's prophecy or usages of this phrase in Luke's account of the Church's growth and expansion. It is not used of the Spirit's coming on the Samaritan converts in Acts 8 or on the Ephesian disciples of John the Baptist in Acts 19. The nearest usage in the rest of the New Testament is found in 1 Corinthians: 'For by one Spirit we were all baptized into one body – Jews or Greeks, slaves or free – and all were made to drink of one Spirit' (1 Cor 12:13).

There are several significant points to note about these six New Testament references:

## Verbal Form

All six references use verbal forms; none use the noun form 'baptism'. Thus there is no biblical instance of the phrase 'baptism in the Holy Spirit'. The exclusive use of the verbal form emphasizes the agent first, and then the instrument used by the agent, more than the experiences of recipients and their consequences. The agent, the one who baptizes with/in the Holy Spirit, is Jesus (in all four gospels; see also Acts 2:33). The instrument or modality is the Spirit.

## Prophetic Context

All the references are prophetic; none are narrative or descriptive. They are either prophetic promises concerning the ministry of Jesus (all four gospels), or prophetic declarations taking up the promise of the Baptist (Acts). John's prophetic word concerning the coming Messiah is twofold: first, that he is 'the lamb of God, who takes away the sin of the world' (John 1:29) and, secondly, that he is the one who will baptize with Holy Spirit. Both statements belong to the core of the Baptist's message as the gospels present it. His role was to prepare the way for the Messiah; this included the prophetic proclamation of the Messiah's distinctive ministry.

The prophetic context embraces both the prophetic promises of the future coming of the Spirit and the first affirmations concerning their fulfilment. The latter are instances of 'This is what was spoken' by the prophets, Joel and John the Baptist (see Acts 2:16; 11:15). These affirmations are themselves prophetic declarations, interpreting in the Spirit the contemporary acts of God.

The absence of the phrase 'baptized in (the) Spirit' from all narrative passages in Acts describing the activity of the Spirit is probably deliberate. The lack of any descriptive use of the phrase 'baptized with/in Holy Spirit' points to the transcendent or meta-empirical character of this prophetic usage. This usage expands the baptismal terminology beyond its empirical ritual meaning to refer to an act of God that is beyond all human measurement. This point confirms the significance of the verbal form; we are dealing with an act of God not with a thing or object.

## Eschatological Gift

The Baptist's prophetic message concerning 'he who is coming' belongs to the tradition of Old Testament prophecy concerning the Messiah and the 'Day of the Lord'. This is most evident from the longer versions in Matthew and Luke, where the expected Messiah will

baptize with fire as well as with Holy Spirit, separating
the wheat for the granary from the chaff to be burned.
In the Old Testament fire is regularly associated with
God's judgment (Lam 2:3–4; Ezek 20:47; Zech 13:9), and
especially with the cataclysmic events at the climax of
history (Isa 66:15; Zeph 1:18; 3:8; Mal 3:2–3). Fire also
represents the absolute holiness of God; 'our God is
a consuming fire' (Heb 12:29) has its background in
Deuteronomy 4 (see vv. 24, 36). The mention of fire
indicates that Jesus' baptismal ministry inaugurates
the last days and is beginning a separating work that
will reach its climax in the final judgment.

The 'fire' element in the Baptist's prophecy has an
affinity with Jesus' description of his death as a 'baptism', a passage that associates the bringing of fire with
Jesus himself: 'I came to cast fire upon the earth; and
would that it were already kindled! I have a baptism
to be baptized with; and how I am constrained until it
is accomplished!' (Luke 12:49–50). Jesus' death is itself
an occasion of judgment, with the manifestation of signs
associated with the end of the world: darkness over the
earth (Matt 27:45; Luke 23:44), earth tremors and the
appearance of the dead (Matt 27:51–53).

The gift of the Spirit at Pentecost was understood as
an eschatological event. In Luke's account in Acts, the
outpouring of the Holy Spirit is an event that both fulfils
prophecy and transforms it. In taking up the prophecy of
Joel, Peter's words add the phrase 'in the last days' (Acts
2:17), thus making explicit the eschatological character of
Joel's prophecy. He also adds 'and they shall prophesy'
to Joel's promise concerning 'my menservants and my
maidservants' (Acts 2:18); this extension of divine blessing beyond Israel also belongs to the 'end-times'.

Like the Old Testament prophets before him, John
the Baptist had no conception of two distinct comings
of the Messiah, separated by the time of the Church. His
perspective is of a single coming associated with the end
of the age, when the Messiah will bring salvation to Israel
and judgment to the nations. The opening up of God's
plan to reveal two comings rather than one leads to the

Messianic promises having two major stages of fulfilment rather than one. In this expansion of vision, the first level of fulfilment becomes a sign of the final and fuller realization of the second coming. So Paul characterizes the gift of the Spirit received by Christians as the 'first fruits of the Spirit' (Rom 8:23), the 'guarantee' or pledge of the future fulness (2 Cor 1:22; 5:5).

Thus we should see the Baptist's prophecy concerning the 'mightier' one who will baptize with Holy Spirit and fire as having at least two levels of fulfilment; one associated with the first coming (at Pentecost and at Caesarea) and a fuller realization at the second coming. Then the greatest outpouring of the Spirit will effect the resurrection of the dead (see Paul's view on the 'great might' of God in raising Jesus in Eph 1:19–20), which will be the full realization of the prophecy of Ezekiel to Israel (Ezek 37:1–14). Here too the first level of fulfilment is a sign and a pledge of the final realization of the prophetic promise.

## Jesus' Heavenly Ministry

The sayings of John the Baptist share the general prophetic vision of God's coming at the end of history;[2] there is no hint of a contemporaneous heavenly world above our earthly existence. In the book of Acts, however, the events of Pentecost and at Caesarea present Jesus' role as baptizer with/in Holy Spirit as a ministry of the glorified and ascended Jesus, now being exercised from heaven.

This heavenly origin and character of Jesus' baptizing with Holy Spirit, hinted at in the narrative account of Pentecost ('suddenly a sound came from heaven' Acts 2:2) is most clearly taught later in the same chapter: 'Being therefore exalted at the right hand of God, and having received from the Father the promise of the Holy Spirit, he has poured out this which you see and hear' (Acts 2:33). For Luke, this baptismal activity of Jesus is the confirming sign of his full mission; because the Holy Spirit has been poured out 'all the house of Israel [can] therefore know assuredly that God has made him both

Lord and Christ, this Jesus whom you crucified' (Acts 2:36).

This heavenly nature of Jesus' ministry as baptizer with/in Holy Spirit may explain why the only fulfilments suggested are the dramatic events of the day of Pentecost in Jerusalem and the 'Gentile Pentecost' at Caesarea. Since this ministry is exercised from heaven, its clearest manifestations are the most evident sovereign interventions of the risen Lord in public corporate settings. Thus, while at Caesarea, unlike Jerusalem, there is the 'horizontal' role of Peter's preaching, the Spirit 'fell on all who heard the word' (Acts 10:44), a description which indicates an element of sovereign invasion. It belongs then to the concept of being baptized with Holy Spirit that the invasion of the Spirit is an experienced intervention of the risen and ascended Jesus. This point will be important when we come to consider the relationship between being baptized with Holy Spirit and the ritual sacramental bath of baptism.[3]

The account in Acts establishes a connection between Jesus' heavenly ministry of pouring out the Spirit and the foundation of the Church. The corporate events of Jerusalem (Acts 2) and Caesarea (Acts 10) demonstrate a truth central to Luke's message that the gospel is universal, destined for both Jews and Gentiles. This is Luke's narrative way of teaching what Paul expresses in Ephesians, that the Church is constituted by the union of Jew and Gentile in the one body (Eph 2:15–16; 3:6). The correlation of the Baptist's prophecy with the foundation of the Church points to Luke's strongly pneumatic view of the Church's nature.

## The Content

The Baptist's prophecy said nothing about the content of being baptized with Holy Spirit (and fire). The transformation of the apostles at Pentecost is indicated more by the contrast in their behaviour after from before, rather than by any specific description of the change. But all the biblical indications are that the gift poured out was the gift of divine life. Spirit is life; when the spirit comes, the dead will live (Ezek 37:6,9,14); when the spirit departs, there is death (Eccl 12:7).

However, with the coming of the Christ we are faced with a higher form of life. 'The life was made manifest, and we saw it, and testify to it, and proclaim to you the eternal life which was with the Father and was made manifest to us' (1 John 1:2). This theme pervades the Johannine writings. This life is no longer the limited forms of physical, biological and psychological life, but the unlimited uncreated life of the eternal God poured into the limited and frail receptacles of human beings. 'I came that they may have life, and have it abundantly' (John 10:10).

This conclusion, that the gift of the Spirit is above all a gift of divine life, is confirmed by the evidence of the transformed disciples. They now preach boldly, they speak confidently and with inner assurance, they risk persecution without fear, they rejoice in suffering for the name of Jesus, they perform signs and wonders, they share their lives and goods with each other. Peter even enters the house of a Gentile! The gift of the Spirit affects every aspect of their lives and every level of their being. The temptation should be resisted to restrict the gift and its meaning to particular effects, however important, whether power, inspiration, or openness to charisms.

## Its Initial Usage in the Pentecostal Movement

The accounts of the origins of the Pentecostal movement indicate that (a) the central blessing was called baptism in the Spirit; and (b) this was understood to be the grace of Pentecost. At Azusa Street this association with Pentecost was so strong that the first issue of their paper *The Apostolic Faith* had the headline 'Pentecost Has Come'. The noun 'Pentecost' was also regularly used of personal reception of 'the baptism', but the corporate sense was significant.

The first Pentecostals believed that this baptism in the Holy Spirit was the recurrence in the twentieth century of the experience of the first Christians. They were convinced that their experience of a second (or even third) blessing subsequent to regeneration–conversion reflected the pattern of Christian experience recorded in the Acts of the Apostles. While Pentecostals undoubtedly did seek to understand the objective data of the New Testament, especially Acts and 1 Corinthians, inevitably perhaps they read back into the Scriptures contemporary patterns of Evangelical and Holiness experience.

It is possible however to recognize that the Pentecostals were led by the Spirit in this identification with Pentecost and their naming of this central experience, without accepting all their exegesis. This can be done by insisting that the original Pentecostal use of the term 'baptism in the Spirit' was primarily prophetic. It is an interpretation of contemporary experience in the light of the Scriptures rather than exegesis of the Scriptures illuminated by present circumstances. The designation of this work as baptism in the Spirit was not simply the result of study of the New Testament, but was a spiritual interpretation and prophetic proclamation that 'This is That' which was spoken of by the prophet Joel and initially experienced on the day of Pentecost.

It is true that at Charles Parham was largely responsible for the teaching that speaking in tongues is the biblical evidence for baptism in the Spirit. He was in the way the father of the doctrine of 'initial evidence' that has characterized the majority of Pentecostals. But it was at Azusa Street that we find the first manifestation of the full range of characteristics that have since marked the world-wide Pentecostal movement: eschatological expectation, restoration of the spiritual gifts, spiritual equipment of every believer, explosive praise, power for evangelism, revelation of the Saviour. Unlike Topeka, it was a public manifestation of the dynamic power of the Spirit reconciling people of different races and sending witnesses throughout the world, whose meaning was most deeply expressed in the prophetic declaration 'This is Pentecost'. In this light, it is significant that the prophetic statement 'This is That' was made in a corporate context, an outpouring of the Spirit on an incredibly diverse gathering of believers at Azusa Street, rather evocative of the diversity recorded in Acts 2.

That the use of the term baptism in the Spirit is primarily prophetic is saying:

- negatively, it is not in its essential reality simply an individual experience located within a series of experiences;
- positively, it refers to a sovereign intervention of God in the life of the Church, and points to a particular work of God at a specific point in Christian history;
- thus a Christian baptized in the Spirit has been plunged by the risen Lord Jesus into the unlimited torrent of the Spirit's life, and thereby participates in a sovereign grace being poured out on the Church; this is understood in faith to be a contemporary experience of the grace that characterized the foundation of the Church and which looks for its completion at the second coming.

## Charismatic Usage

From the beginning of the charismatic movement, participants readily used the Spirit-baptism terminology of the Pentecostals. The dominant Pentecostal doctrine concerning baptism in the Spirit was criticized from opposite angles – from the Evangelical side, by those insisting on the simultaneity of regeneration and the gift of the Spirit; from the Catholic side, by those concerned to uphold baptismal regeneration and the objective gift of the Spirit in the sacraments of initiation.

Despite the theological objections, the majority stuck, perhaps somewhat obstinately, to the terminology of baptism in the Spirit. If this prophetic interpretation is correct, such obstinacy could represent a tenacity of the Spirit in the face of powerful pressures, both doctrinal and pastoral. It no doubt represented a deep instinct that this was an appropriate term, despite the real difficulties raised by Church leaders and theologians. This sense of its appropriateness probably flowed from an awareness of the link between this contemporary grace and the event of Pentecost. The charismatic movement with its eruption in almost every Christian tradition appeared as an outpouring of the Spirit 'on all flesh' as prophesied by Joel and applied in Acts 2:17. Humanly speaking, the extent of this usage owed much to the distinctive ministry of David du Plessis.

From 1959, du Plessis circled the world announcing this outpouring of the Spirit on Christians of every Church and every continent. Central to his message was Jesus' role as baptizer with the Spirit and the identity of this blessing with the earlier Pentecostal outpouring. What Christians in the mainline Churches are experiencing, he announced, is the baptism in the Holy Spirit, the same grace as the Lord poured out at Azusa Street. Just as the Pentecostal usage of Spirit-baptism was prophetic, so David du Plessis' distinctive ministry was prophetic. He embodied the essential link between identification of this grace as baptism in the Spirit and affirmation of its universal and unitive character. Du Plessis grasped the importance of the same term being used to describe the central grace common to all streams.

## The Significance of being Baptized in the Holy Spirit Today

If this reflection is on the right lines, the significance of the Pentecostal and charismatic movements lies above all in two related points: (a) the sovereign manner of God's action through the risen Jesus baptizing with/in Holy Spirit and (b) the heavenly uncreated character of the life poured out. Just as the events of Pentecost and Caesarea gave the primitive Church a strong sense of the eschatological and heavenly character of the Church and of the Christian life, so this outpouring of the Holy Spirit in the twentieth century is restoring to the Church a dynamic faith in, and a direct knowledge of, the risen and glorified Lord who, bearing the wounds of Calvary, pours out from the divine throne streams of living water.

This Pentecostal–charismatic faith knows an immediacy of relationship to the persons of the Trinity, and knows too that the Spirit gives a taste of the good things of the coming kingdom. While the prophetic identification of this outpouring leads Pentecostal and charismatic Christians to see this contemporary movement in terms of restoration of New Testament Christianity (intensity of faith expectation, manifestation and availability of spiritual gifts and empowered ministries), it is a mistake to interpret it wholly in relation to the past. As Pentecost was the initial fulfilment of the Baptist's prophecy, so the second coming will be its final fulfilment. Intermediate sovereign outpourings of the Spirit look forward as much as back. They are of their nature a preparation for the second coming. So an essential element of the significance of this contemporary move is that the risen Lord is raising the Church up to a higher level of faith-life so that the Church can play its proper role in preparing for the second coming. How this compares to the faith-level of the primitive Church is impossible to judge and not the most essential point.

The spiritual gifts which are evidently a distinguishing feature of the Pentecostal–charismatic outpouring are best seen, not as the essence of the phenomenon, but as characteristic signs of the divine sovereign intervention of baptizing with Holy Spirit. For all the spiritual gifts (*charismata pneumatika*) of 1 Corinthians 12:8–10, unlike gifts such as celibacy (1 Cor 7:7) and those listed in Romans 12:6–8 with the exception of prophecy, require in their original and authentic expression a surrender of the human mind and will to the sovereign action of the Lord. This view explains how the spiritual gifts always characterize the Pentecostal and charismatic movements without becoming their essence and focal point.

This contemporary grace of God directly addresses our present spiritual malaise. To a Church in which many people hardly believe that God acts in any identifiable

way, or who think that such direct manifestations of
God's love and mercy are reserved for the few or for
the past, this current of divine life is a clear sign that
'Jesus Christ is the same yesterday and today and
for ever' (Heb 13:8). The sense that the Church is on
the defensive, constantly yielding ground to secularist
trends, her influence ever more ineffective, is strikingly
reversed by this sovereign manifestation of divine life
and power. The increasing restriction of Christian life
to a private sphere with minimal impact on the world is
dramatically challenged by the public character of these
outpourings and the communities and ministries to which
they give rise.

# CHAPTER SIX

# UNDERSTANDING BAPTISM IN THE SPIRIT

The Pentecostal and charismatic movements represent a mighty initiative of the Lord. However, their
histories are not simply tales of grace and triumph, but
have been marked by major ambiguities. This makes
it necessary to distinguish between the grace poured
out by the Lord and what Pentecostal and charismatic
Christians have done with it.

What Christians have done with this torrent of grace
has many dimensions: doctrinal, governmental, cultic-
liturgical, pastoral, ecclesial. Crucial to this human
response is the understanding of the central grace of baptism in the Spirit. It is the adequacy of our understanding
that will determine whether we do justice to the size and
scope of the grace received. If we do not understand it in
faith and in depth, there is little possibility of this grace
bearing its appointed fruit.

The question then is whether Pentecostal and charismatic understandings of baptism in the Spirit have done
justice to the gift. Here a key principle must be stated:
*acts of God require divine light to understand them.*
This principle is all the more applicable to movements
originating as sovereign interventions of the Lord in
ways that are not initially dependent on human founders.
Experience of the act of God must lead to interaction with
the Scriptures in reverent quest for light on its content
and meaning. This principle contests the assumption that
the meaning of baptism in the Spirit is obvious – that it is
simply more power for a powerless Church, restoration of

the charisms, restoration or renewal of the Church, where
our ideas of power, of restoration, of Church, remain
largely what they were before. In fact, such assumptions
betray an arrogance that fails to recognize the limitations
of the human mind faced with the mysterious workings of
the infinite God.

# The Pentecostal Movement

## Background

The first Pentecostals were heirs to more than a century
of seeking a post-conversion blessing designated the
baptism in/with the Holy Spirit. From the time of John
Fletcher of Madeley (1729–1785), one of John Wesley's
most trusted associates, first some Methodists, later also
some Presbyterians, sought to identify and receive this
blessing. First conceived in terms of personal sanctification, baptism in the Spirit came to be seen in some late
nineteenth-century circles as an empowerment for ministry. These milieux are normally seen as the immediate
antecedents for the Pentecostal understanding of baptism
in the Spirit. The history of the evolution of this term has
been chronicled by several scholars.[1]

Throughout this development, the presuppositions were
that individual Christians were seeking (a) the fulness
of the Holy Spirit in their personal lives and ministry
and (b) the normative patterns for Christian initiation
and perfection according to the New Testament. Not
surprisingly, these two were closely related in practice,
so that the theology of the seekers was clearly marked by
their personal experience. The origins of the Pentecostal
usage and understanding are commonly understood as
a further step in this search and discovery. What is
insufficiently noticed is that the Pentecostal usage is
not simply an evolution in individual wrestling with
spiritual growth in the light of the biblical text, but
represents something decisively new. The newness is
that in the Pentecostal movement the term has become
the prophetic interpretation of a public event.

If the developments associated with Charles Parham

had not been followed by the outbreak at Azusa Street, the former would probably only have been another variant on the interpretation of baptism in the Spirit as an individual Christian experience. It would have had no greater claim to validity than many other interpretations of individual experience in Holiness circles – probably less as Parham seems to have been less impressive as a theologian and as a Christian leader than men like Charles G. Finney and Asa Mahan. It was the dynamic birth of the Pentecostal revival symbolized by Azusa Street that was new. The claim that 'This is Pentecost' was an interpretation of this public event that was of significance for the whole Church.

Azusa Street, Los Angeles, was the main focus for this Pentecostal outpouring of the Spirit that spread so rapidly across the world. The news from Azusa sparked most of the other centres of Pentecostal revival.[2] The corporate sense spreading from Azusa Street was much enhanced by the characteristically Afro-American corporate sense of being a people under God. This difference is important when comparisons are made between Azusa Street and earlier revivals in the Evangelical world.

## Pentecostal self-understanding

Among Pentecostals, there has been from the beginning an inner tension between the individual believer's growth in the Spirit and the sense of a divine intervention of import for the whole world. This tension leads to a dichotomy between the significance attributed to the Pentecostal movement as a whole and the meaning given to baptism in the Spirit. The whole movement is seen as a divine intervention for the Church and the world, but baptism in the Spirit continues to be seen in the framework of individual blessing.

The earliest Pentecostal understanding of baptism in the Spirit is best grasped from testimonies, which abound in all their broadsheets and magazines. The Azusa magazine, *Apostolic Faith*, published countless witnesses to the Spirit's remarkable work in that ramshackle backstreet shed. As this move of the Spirit spread, witnesses multiplied. The harmony of these witnesses to the same work of the Spirit is impressive. One of the first attempts to formulate the meaning and effects of baptism in the Spirit was the London Declaration drawn up by about thirty British Pentecostal leaders in 1909. Under the heading 'What we teach concerning the Evidence and the Results' they state:

*The Sign of Tongues*. The 'promise of the Father' (Acts 1:4) was, and is, evidenced by the Speaking in 'Tongues' as the Spirit gives to utter (see Acts 2:4, Greek; also Acts 10:46, and 19:6).

But it also includes:

*Seven Results*
1st   The Consciousness of the Deity of our Lord Jesus Christ (John 14:20).
2nd   The Consciousness of our 'Dwelling in Him' (1 John 3:23, 24) and He in us (Eph 3:17).
3rd   Divine Illumination concerning His Word and Will (John 14:16, 17).
4th   'The Testimony of Jesus' (Rev 19:10; John 15:26, 27). The Lord Jesus said that, after receiving this Promise, 'Ye shall be witnesses unto Me' (Acts 1:8).
5th   The Three-fold Conviction of the World by the Spirit in us. ('I will send the Comforter to you, and when He is come He will reprove the World of Sin, of Righteousness, and of Judgment' John 16:8–11).
  – The great Sin of fallen man (his unbelief).
  – The need of the Righteousness of Christ (now with His Father).
  – The Judgment of the Devil (Heb 2:14,15). [The Prince of the World is already condemned.]
6th   Our continual guidance into the deep things of God (John 16:13; 1 Cor 2:9,10).
7th   The continual glorification of Christ (to the exclusion of self) John 16:14; Eph 1:17–23; Col 2:15, 3:3).

It is also clear from Holy Scripture (Heb 2:4) that God
bears witness both with signs and wonders, and with
divers miracles, and distributions of the Holy Ghost,
according to His own will. (See also Mark 16:19,20;
John 14:11,12). . . .
It also should be clearly understood that the Baptism
of the Holy Ghost is the 'Gate' into, and not the
'Goal' of a true and full Christian life.[3]

While this declaration shares the individualist presuppositions of the nineteenth-century Holiness debate, it is
a wonderfully comprehensive summary of the blessings
received by the Christian baptized in the Spirit. It is
striking in its clear focus on the person of Jesus. The
Spirit bears witness to Jesus, the Spirit reveals the
person and work of Jesus, the Spirit glorifies Jesus,
and the Spirit convicts of all that is opposed to the
righteousness of God embodied in Jesus.

It is interesting to notice what is not in the declaration. There is no reference to stages or phases in
the Christian life. There is no emphasis on power; the
gifts are listed as the 'Manifestation of the Spirit'.[4] The
London Declaration was drawn up before any Pentecostal
denominations had been formed in Britain. The formation
of denominations led inevitably to the formulation of
official doctrine. Seeing the centrality of baptism in
the Spirit in the Pentecostal experience, it was natural
that new statements of faith should express convictions
concerning baptism in the Spirit. However, this process
involved a narrowing of focus so that the only aspects
of baptism in the Spirit specified in official Pentecostal
statements of faith are some or all of the following: (a) the
evidence for its reception (commonly seen as speaking in
tongues); (b) its distinction from conversion-regeneration;
(c) enduement with power; (d) bestowal of the spiritual
gifts. Unlike the London Declaration, the foundational
statements of faith of Pentecostal Churches ordinarily
make no reference to important, and indeed central,
components of this work of God, as for example: (a) an
immediacy of relationship to the persons of the Trinity;

(b) the doors of revelation being opened; (c) the capacity to praise God with a new directness and freedom of expression.

A well-known Pentecostal writer, Stanley Frodsham, wrote in 1909: 'The Pentecostal Baptism of the Holy Spirit brings a deeper and clearer revelation of our Lord and Saviour, Jesus Christ.'[5] A Pentecostal failure to grasp the greatness of the 'baptism' is reproached in a sermon by pioneer missionary John G. Lake:

> The common teaching that my heart these days is endeavoring to combat is that God comes to present the individual with a gift of power, and the individual is then supposed to go out and manifest some certain characteristic of power. No! God comes to present you with Himself. 'You shall receive power after that the Holy Ghost is come upon you.' Jesus went to heaven in order that the very treasury of the heart of the eternal God might be unlocked for your benefit and that out of the very soul of the eternal God, the streams of His life and nature would possess you from the crown of your head to the sole of your feet.[6]

## Charismatic Renewal

Did charismatic Christians understand being baptized in the Spirit any differently when this grace of Pentecost spread beyond the ranks of the Pentecostals from the 1950s? There is certainly a difference of atmosphere from Azusa Street, but the effects of baptism in the Spirit are remarkably consistent.

So, for example, an Anglican baptized in the Spirit in the first years of charismatic renewal testified:

> Then it hit me – total submission to Him! All of a sudden my hands went up as though I had no control – all the way up! At the same time the Lord Jesus baptized me in His Spirit. When I raised my hands it was like diving into water. I could feel God's presence

from the top of my finger tips, coming down over my arms, over my head – complete immersion in the Lord. Praise in the gift of tongues flowed freely up to God. More satisfying than all the accumulated honours of many years, God's love that night surpassed anything I had ever known. Ever since that night, the Bible and Prayer Book have become living words to me as well as the desire to serve my Lord in my local parish or wherever He places me. To love and serve Jesus Christ, is fulfilment, joy unspeakable, and real life.[7]

Charismatic Christians in the mainline Churches did not experience the need to draw up statements of faith, because they saw themselves as loyal members of their Churches and upholders of their historic Creeds and confessions of faith. They experienced baptism in the Spirit as giving new life and vitality to these historic truths. Two features in particular distinguished them from the Pentecostals: (a) the imposition of hands to receive the 'baptism' and the abandonment of 'tarrying' for the Spirit to come[8]; and (b) relating their charismatic experience to their traditional theologies of Christian initiation. In addition, the Catholic charismatics quickly developed programmes or seminars to prepare candidates to be baptized in the Spirit, a practice that has become almost universal in Catholic charismatic renewal and that has spread among other renewal circles, particularly the Anglicans.

The theological reflections focused not surprisingly on the legitimacy of the charismatic experience. Evangelicals sought to demonstrate the scriptural basis for affirming a baptism in the Spirit subsequent to regeneration-conversion, which often produced more sophisticated versions of the Pentecostal empowerment teaching. Catholic writings, along with those of other Christians of more sacramental traditions, naturally sought to relate the baptism in the Spirit to the sacraments of initiation that impart the Holy Spirit according to classical Catholic teaching. It was generally assumed to be obvious what

baptism in the Spirit meant, so the theological task
was to accommodate this to traditional doctrines; as
a result insufficient attention was paid to the ways in
which it transcends and challenges received theologies
and practice.

Of course these are generalizations, and there were
signs and hints of deeper reflection. Among Catholics,
the first Malines document of 1974 did begin its analysis
of the theological basis of the charismatic renewal with
sections on (a) the inner life of the Trinity and experience;
(b) Christ and the Holy Spirit; and (c) the Church and the
Holy Spirit.[9] This perspective could have prepared the
way for a more total presentation of the gift of Pentecost.
One limitation has been that most theologians have not
been living in the thick of the renewal, where daily
experience reinforces the full challenge of the Spirit,
while the pastoral leaders have been so absorbed with the
demands of ministry that deeper reflection often appears
an impossible luxury.

## Towards a More Adequate Theological Understanding of Baptism in the Spirit

From what has been said so far, especially in Chapter
Five and so far in Chapter Six, the key elements that need
to be brought together in any theological understanding
of baptism in the Spirit include the following:

(1)   the relationship between the visibly invasive
character of the two events to which the term is indi-
rectly applied in the New Testament and the experienced immediacy of the divine persons in contemporary
Pentecostal-charismatic circles;

(2)   the role of the risen and ascended Lord Jesus as
baptizer in/with Holy Spirit;

(3)   the 'one baptism' of Ephesians 4:5;

(4)   the relationship between the eschatological context of the New Testament usage and the significance of
the Pentecostal-charismatic outpouring in the twentieth
century;

(5)   the relationship between the prophetic meta-empirical language of 'baptized in Spirit' in the New Testament and the narrative-descriptive usage describing the rites of Christian initiation;

(6)   the ecumenical or trans-confessional character of the twentieth-century event to which the biblical terminology of 'baptized in Spirit' has been prophetically applied.

Taking these six points seriously can help us to avoid the problems created on the one hand by collapsing baptism in the Spirit into ritual initiation, whether Evangelical conversion or Catholic baptism-confirmation, and on the other hand by positing two baptisms, one in water and one in Spirit, in the manner of the Pentecostals. The key appears to lie in the difference between the New Testament usage of 'baptized in Holy Spirit' and its references to baptism in water. This difference is found in the prophetic character of the former and the narrative-descriptive usage in the latter.

If this interpretation is correct, it means that there is a deliberate refusal in the New Testament to equate the two languages and references. This is not to say that there is not a necessary relationship between them. The language of 'baptized in Holy Spirit' is restricted to manifest sovereign interventions of the Lord that cannot be reduced or limited to any ritual action. This corporate experience of the Church's initial formation remains a paradigm for all subsequent Christian initiation. The eruptive-invasive character of Pentecost demonstrates the heavenly origin and immediacy of relationship that is also true, but not so visibly, of the work of the Holy Spirit that is mediated through the preached Word and the enacted Word of sacramental action.

The grace of Pentecost is signified in the liturgies of Christian initiation which are celebrated in faith. The sign always points to the fulness of redemption in the final kingdom, whereas the spiritual blessing received from its celebration varies enormously from one instance to another. The variants obviously include: the faith of the recipients, the faith of the congregation, the teaching preceding the celebration.

The Pentecostal-charismatic outpouring of this century thus confronts all Christians with: (a) the heavenly origin and character of the gift of the Spirit; (b) the immediacy of relationship in the Spirit between the Christian and the three divine persons in the one God; (c) the present lordship and sovereign rule of the risen and ascended Christ. The statement that Jesus is the one who baptizes with Holy Spirit expresses these three elements.

This claim is of course deeply shocking to many contemporary Christians; the more secularized our mentality, the more shocking it is. It is also deeply disturbing to all those insisting on the structures of mediation by which Christian faith has been handed down to us; both to the Evangelical insisting above all on the mediation of the Word of God and of expository preaching, and to the Catholic insisting on the mediation of liturgy and sacrament, of priestly ministry and apostolic succession.

Later chapters in this book will examine the relationship between divine interventions and embodiment in history. At this point, it is only necessary to insist that God has appointed historic structures of mediation, and that Christians cannot ignore them by an appeal to divine interventions and directness of access to God in the Spirit. It is our task to relate the immediate and the mediated, the heavenly and the historically incarnate, in a way that respects all the data of the New Testament. The unity of the Church as the body of Christ depends on the interaction of the immediate and the mediated, the Spirit and the body. Without the Spirit poured out from heaven, the Church is no more than a religious institution and heritage. Without embodiment in historical forms and instruments, there could be spiritual dynamics but no body of Christ.

The sovereign transcendent character of Jesus' heavenly ministry as baptizer in Holy Spirit makes possible the totally trans-confessional character of the Pentecostal-charismatic current of life, and grounds the depth of its challenge to all Christian Churches and traditions.

For the possibility of transforming revival and renewal is dependent upon the proper subordination of all the structures of mediation to the sovereign freedom and promises of the Blessed Trinity.

## Conclusion

A fuller theological account of being baptized in the Spirit would follow these lines. The baptism in the Holy Spirit is a sovereign outpouring of the Spirit of God, by the risen and ascended Jesus, upon the people of God through which the Lord equips the Church to fulfil its essential mission in preparing for the second coming of Jesus. This outpouring brings new life to all that is of the Spirit in each Church inheritance, and restores elements that have been neglected and forgotten. Through this grace of Pentecost renewed, Christians experience as 'first-fruits' on earth what they will receive in fulness at the Parousia. This brings:

(1)   an immediacy of relationship to the Triune God, that reveals in the human spirit the person of Jesus as Saviour and Lord, the presence and power of the Holy Spirit as well as the majesty and merciful love of the Father;

(2)   a corresponding immediacy upward to God in worship that makes possible spontaneous expression of praise, especially in the speech of tongues that expresses the human spirit without the mediation of the mind;

(3)   an immediacy in the downward relationship of God to the Christian, that makes possible a reception of divine communication in the human spirit;

(4)   a power of the Spirit to love, minister and serve both the community of the faithful and the world outside the Church in evangelization and service;

(5)   the bestowal and the renewal of particular spiritual and ministerial gifts for the effective realization of the Lord's mission.

# CHAPTER SEVEN

# PENTECOST AND PAROUSIA

Pentecostal–charismatic Christianity is generally characterized by heightened expectation of the return of
the Lord. As indicated in Chapter Five, baptism in the
Spirit has an essential reference to the second coming
and awakens Christians to this widely neglected aspect of
Christian faith. This chapter will bring this eschatological
dimension into sharper focus.

## The Pentecostal Movement

The beginnings of the Pentecostal movement were strongly
marked by a sense of the approaching end, and the urgent
need to preach the message of 'Pentecost' throughout
the world before the Lord's return. At Azusa Street,
the refrain 'Jesus is coming soon' accompanied the news
that 'Pentecost has come'. In the first decade of the
Pentecostal movement, greater prominence was given to
the second coming than to speaking in tongues.

One of the main designations given to the new movement, the 'Latter Rain', itself pointed to the soon-coming
of the Lord. This language picked up biblical references
to the autumn and spring rains in Palestine, especially
Joel 2:23 and James 5:7, applying them to outpourings
of the Holy Spirit.[1] For the Pentecostals, the early rain
referred to Pentecost and the origins of the Church,
while the latter rain which ripens the harvest is the
outpouring of the Spirit at the end of the ages. While
Latter Rain advocates generally had a very negative view
of Christianity from the fourth century to the sixteenth,
Latter Rain terminology only strictly implies: (a) that

this Pentecostal outpouring represents a similar *pattern* of blessing to that of the origins and (b) the proximity of the Lord's return.

Early Pentecostal sermons often associated the restoration of the charismata with ardent expectation of the Parousia. That Pentecostals saw an essential connection between the baptism in the Spirit and the return of the Lord is indicated by the 'Foursquare' titles they ascribed to Jesus: Saviour, Baptizer in the Spirit, Healer and Coming King. The second and the fourth titles bring out this connection, that the Lord who baptizes in the Holy Spirit is also the Coming King. Early Pentecostal periodicals reflected this eschatological hope in their message and some in their titles, such as *Bridal Call*, *The Bridegroom's Messenger*, and *The Midnight Cry*.

## Charismatic Revival

The tight link between baptism in the Spirit and heightened expectation of the second coming can be tested by the eschatological consciousness in the charismatic movement. In other words, Pentecostal excitement about the Lord's imminent return may have been caused by factors other than baptism in the Spirit – for example, belonging to a revivalistic tradition, the sociological milieu of early Pentecostals, all that is expressed in the title of Robert Mapes Anderson's study, *Vision of the Disinherited*.[2] The spread of baptism in the Spirit and spiritual gifts to other Christian milieux, theologically and sociologically different, can act as a test: is the connection between baptism in the Spirit and intensified hope for the Parousia incidental or essential?

Significant here is the witness of French Reformed pastor Louis Dallière (1897–1976), the founder of the Union de Prière of Charmes-sur-Rhône launched in 1946. He was the first 'charismatic theologian' in the sense of a Christian scholar in an older Church tradition, baptized in the Spirit and articulating the Pentecostal experience in a non-revivalist theological framework. For Dallière, the heart of the Pentecostal movement was the restoration of a living-faith desire for Jesus' second coming. His contribution will be examined in more detail in Chapter Eleven.

Even before the beginnings of the charismatic renewal as a recognizable movement distinct from the world of the Pentecostals, there was an outbreak of spiritual gifts and charismatic phenomena in a German Lutheran milieu. This occurred among a group of young women, who became the nucleus of a new religious community, the Mary Sisters in Darmstadt, led by Mother Basilea Schlink. From their origins at the end of World War II, the Darmstadt sisters had a particular longing for the second coming, and sensed a calling to a 'bridal love for Jesus'. Schlink wrote of those days: 'The shining of the City of God made us want Jesus to prepare us for the goal of glory, for the Marriage of the Lamb, no matter what the cost.'[3]

Since the visible rise of the charismatic movement in the 1960s, there have been numerous signs of heightened eschatological expectation. Several communities and prayer groups have called themselves *Maranatha*. Many songs of the renewal look forward to the Lord's return, e.g. 'The Spirit and the Bride' and 'Lion of Judah on the throne'. Books on this subject have appeared in Church circles not influenced by fundamentalist debates on millennial themes, such as Ralph Martin's *The Return of the Lord*.[4] A major French charismatic community, *La communauté du Lion de Juda et de l'Agneau Immolé*,[5] states in its Book of Life: 'In these times, which are the last, the Lord sends forth his consoling Spirit to renew his Church, so that she may present herself as his Spouse and so that he may invite her to the banquet of the Lamb.' This community document continues:

Riveted by this eschatological reality and fascinated by the perfection of the world to come, the Community sighs and groans with all of Creation in a watchful and unending prayer; she proclaims, by her life, in a way both implicit and explicit, the reality of the kingdom and the imminence of its coming; she anticipates, by means of a life of loving relations

among members of God's family, by means of the
sacramental life, by means of worship and liturgy,
the kingdom's coming.

While charismatic circles within the mainline Church
traditions have not exhibited the heart-felt longing for
the end that characterized early Pentecostalism, there
is widespread evidence that they had been awakened
through baptism in the Spirit to an awareness of the
coming heavenly kingdom not possessed by the aver-
age Church member. The lower general intensity no
doubt reflects the more comfortable social conditions
widely enjoyed by the 'neo-Pentecostals'. The language
of *renewal* itself points to a greater concern for ongoing
Church life in this world. This eschatological hope is most
vivid in renewal milieux where the Lord's grace has been
taken with the greatest seriousness.

## The Meaning of this Link

This link in the Pentecostal and charismatic movements
between the revival of spiritual gifts and the longing
for eschatological fulfilment cannot be merely coinci-
dental. Some seventy-five years before the beginnings of
the Pentecostal movement, the noted Scottish preacher,
Edward Irving, had written of the gift of tongues:

> And I would say, that this gift hath ceased to be
> visible in the Church, because of her great ignorance
> concerning that work of Christ at His second coming,
> of which it is the continual sign; because of her
> most culpable ignorance of Christ's crowned glory,
> of which it is the continual demonstration; because of
> her indifference to the world without, for preaching
> to which the gift of the Holy Ghost is the continual
> furnishing and outfit of the Church.[6]

First, the spiritual gifts make heaven more real. The
reappearance of the full range of these gifts make more
evident the *heavenly* character of the kingdom of God.

The gifts called *pneumatika* (spiritual) differ from other charismata, such as hospitality and administration, in requiring for their exercise a faith in the present power of the risen Lord. They are not simply a heightening of human talents in the service of the kingdom, but have their origin 'from above'.

The spiritual gifts demonstrate the reality of our heavenly destiny. They represent a particular form of 'first fruits', of the Christian experiencing on earth a foretaste of heaven. Of their nature, they communicate knowledge and enkindle desire for the full realization of the final kingdom. Thus a strong hope for the Parousia only seems to grow and deepen in those milieux where the spiritual gifts continue to be exercised.

Secondly, the spiritual gifts are dependent on the resurrection and ascension of Christ. They are poured out by the Lord Jesus from the right hand of the Father (see Acts 2:33). 'Therefore it is said, "When he ascended on high he led a host of captives, and he gave gifts to men"' (Eph 4:8). They depend on the proclamation of Jesus' victory over sin, Satan and death. Inner yielding to the Lord to receive and exercise these gifts deepens faith in Jesus' victory, and leads to a greater awareness of the fulness of that victory that will be manifested in the resurrection of the dead and the final defeat of death.

Here too Edward Irving had some striking comments about the spiritual gifts as a share in Jesus' glorified humanity:

> The miracle-workers in the Church are Christ's hand, to shew the strength that is in Him: the healers of diseases are His almoners, to shew what pity and compassion are in Him: the faith-administrators are His lion-heart, to shew how mighty and fearless He is: and the utterers of wisdom and knowledge are His mind, to shew how rich and capacious it is. They do all contain, and exhibit and minister to the world, some portion of that fulness which is in Him, and which He alone is capable of holding in one subsistence.[7]

Thirdly, the reappearance of the spiritual gifts involves a restoration of revelation in the Spirit. Pentecostal and charismatic witnesses constantly speak of hearing the Lord, of receiving a word, of having an inner sense, etc. The fact that people can be mistaken, and that all such communication requires discernment, does not destroy the credibility of these claims. For the counterfeit only appears in the context of the real thing.

Revelation in the Spirit means the direct communication of divine things to the human spirit. There is an unveiling of heavenly knowledge, of how God sees things. Through the Holy Spirit, the Lord reveals inwardly to the believer what was outwardly revealed in Jesus Christ two thousand years ago. It does not add to the revelation in Jesus, but represents the Spirit taking what belongs to Jesus and declaring it to Christians in the present (John 16:15).

This elevation of the Christian in the spirit bestows an affinity for the *eschata*, for the kingdom to be fully inaugurated and unveiled with the return of Christ. Because the heavenly Christ is revealed and known, Christians desire full union with the heavenly spouse they love, and long for the full realization of God's saving purpose. Christians filled with the Holy Spirit will be able to pray 'Maranatha; come Lord Jesus' as the spontaneous desire of the heart.

An intensified longing for the second coming of Jesus is then an essential fruit of the outpouring of the Holy Spirit in the Pentecostal and charismatic movements. It is a grace for the Church, so that the whole people of God may know their inheritance, and long for its fulfilment. 'Come, Lord Jesus', is not just the prayer of the pious and other-worldly Christian, but the heartfelt cry of the pilgrim Church. It is the prayer of the 'groaning creation' that is in travail (Rom 8:22); it is the prayer of those who know 'the first fruits of the Spirit' and 'groan inwardly as we wait for adoption as sons, the redemption of our bodies' (Rom 8:23).

Fourthly, the charismata play their full role only in the context of strong corporate expressions of Church life. It

is significant that the eschatological hope was notably
stronger at Azusa Street. Similarly, we find that the
strongest expressions of longing for the wedding feast of
the Lamb in the charismatic movement occurred in committed communities honouring the charism of celibacy,[8]
which in the New Testament has a direct eschatological
significance (see 1 Cor 7:25–31). Because human communion is mediated through the body, the fulness of
communion in Christ requires the resurrection of the
body. Only a strong corporate faith is likely to sustain
a living hope for the second coming and the resurrection
of the dead.

# CHAPTER EIGHT

# GREATER UNITY OR MORE DIVISION?

Nowhere is the ambiguity of the Pentecostal–charismatic phenomenon more evident than in the issue of unity and division. The glory is manifested in the powerful reconciling and unitive thrust of baptism in the Spirit, while shame attaches to the pettiness of the quarrels and the scandals of constant division.

In the beginnings of the Pentecostal movement, the unifying power of the Holy Spirit was vividly experienced. Those baptized in the Spirit knew they had new life within them, and they experienced a deep bond of kinship with others who knew this new life. What each had received personally was shared with others. They could praise God spontaneously, and they could do so together. They could speak and sing in other tongues individually, and they could do it together. They could now speak the Word to others with power, and recognize the power of the Word in them. This combination of newness of life and communion with others grounded their deep sense of spiritual unity. This experienced unity in the Spirit gave rise to a vision of the unity of all believers. Several Pentecostal pioneers were strongly impressed by this vision, so that Christian unity featured prominently in the preaching of Frank Bartleman of Los Angeles, Alexander Boddy of Sunderland, W. Hamner Piper of Chicago and W. F. Carothers from Houston.

But the actual history of the Pentecostal movement represents more disappointment in this respect than a transmission of this hope for Christian unity. Each decade of Pentecostalism has experienced divisiveness and seen further schisms. New denominations have continued to proliferate at an astonishing rate. Many stem from quarrels and conflicts between leaders; fewer have a doctrinal origin. Many represent the ethos of capitalist competition operative in the sphere of religion.

By its fifth decade the Pentecostal movement had virtually lost any unitive vision. Apart from notable exceptions such as Donald Gee and David du Plessis, the leaders had largely accepted the inevitability of denominational multiplicity and idealized the spirit of independence. Moreover, the Pentecostals had bought into an aggressive opposition to the mainline Churches, which were seen as at best moribund, at worst apostate. The ecumenical movement was rejected as a 'man-made' attempt at Church unity in contrast to the God-given unity of the Spirit-baptized.

## New Hope for Unity

In this context, the second surprise, the spread of pentecostal blessing to the historic Protestant Churches, elicited a new surge of ecumenical hope. Once again there was an excitement among those baptized in the Spirit that the Spirit was bridging age-old divides; a power was at work to undermine and demolish the walls of separation. This sense was strongly accentuated by the third surprise, the spread to the Roman Catholics. While the Catholic extension posed greater problems of authenticity for all Pentecostals, it heightened awareness that something of momentous import was happening.

In fact this wave of new hope for unity in the early years of the charismatic movement was greater than at the time of Azusa Street. For, unlike the Pentecostal beginnings, the charismatic revival was touching Christians of practically every Church tradition, and they were frequently being blessed through each other. It is remarkable how many charismatic pioneers came into this pentecostal

blessing through contact with Christians of other traditions. With the wide range of traditions implicated, the
new-found fellowship regularly extended to Christians
previously unknown and beyond the range of conceivable
communion.

This spread of charismatic renewal to Christians in
the mainline Churches pierced the barriers surrounding Pentecostal fellowship. Many Anglicans, Lutherans,
Reformed, Methodists and Catholics baptized in the
Spirit were Christians already open to the idea of wider
Christian fellowship, and in some cases deeply dedicated
to the original ecumenical vision of spiritual reconciliation and organic unity. Many instinctively sensed the
immense potential of this new move of the Spirit for
Christian unity.

In the early 1970s, it was possible to look at the
nascent charismatic renewal, and experience a real hope
for dramatic steps towards Christian unity. The new tide
of the charismatic movement could be seen as reversing
the earlier Pentecostal tendency towards division into
new denominations. Whereas the older Churches had
not been ready for this gift in the first decade of this
century, perhaps sixty or seventy years later they would
be open to receive it. So the unitive potential of baptism
in the Spirit would finally become manifest.

## Major Barriers Transcended

The sense of something momentous occurring arose especially from this work of the Spirit bridging the Reformation divide. Not in four hundred years of division
in the Western Church had there been a grass-roots
revival movement involving both Protestants and Roman
Catholics. The momentousness of this break-through was
further underlined by the positive reception generally
accorded to the charismatic renewal by the Catholic
authorities, especially the welcome of Pope Paul VI in
1975.

This exciting break-through also involved the bridging
of another gap that had been widening in recent decades; between the older liturgical–confessional–ecumenical

Churches and the Evangelical/Holiness/Pentecostal world arising out of the revival currents of the last 250 years.

In recent decades, the fastest-growing Christian groups have been either Evangelical or Pentecostal–charismatic, especially the latter. The older Churches for whom Church identity is important, with their commitment to historic creeds, confessions and liturgies, were being thrown on the defensive, and losing ground in many countries of the West. This opposition between the older Churches and the revivalist currents, was often associated with other tensions – between the historically-conscious and non-historical fundamentalists, between liberals and conservatives.

The spread of the charismatic renewal to the older liturgical and credal or confessional Churches represented a significant breach in this newer barrier. Theologians and biblical scholars were among those baptized in the Spirit in the early years of charismatic renewal. This too gave rise to hope for significant break-throughs in the areas of biblical exegesis, of theology, of Church history, of an ecumenical vision for the Church.

## Twenty-Five Years Later

In the 1990s, it is impossible to be so optimistic as in the early 1970s. Some countries in which charismatic renewal began with a strongly ecumenical flavour have seen a regression into more tightly-knit Church groupings. The excitement of the Spirit bridging centuries-old barriers has given way to sentiments favouring retrenchment. Other Christians are found to be other still, despite the euphoria of charismatic embraces. In Ireland, where the beginning had a strongly ecumenical character (it was the only country whose national service committee originally included Catholics and Protestants), this dimension has almost entirely disappeared. This is especially tragic in a land in which any authentic ecumenical witness has a special poignancy and power. In Latin America, very few traces remain of the ecumenical origins of the charismatic renewal among Catholics, sparked off by the visits of inter-church teams to several countries bewtween 1970 and 1972.

Despite the considerable degree of charismatic fellowship and contact across the big divides, older attitudes of suspicion and rejection die hard. The Roman Catholic Church, faced by the extraordinary explosion of Pentecostalism in Latin America, sees the issues primarily in terms of the 'invasion of the sects'. Many Evangelical and Pentecostal missionary agencies still refuse to accept the Christian character of the Catholic Church and work to rescue the Catholic people from the darkness of superstition and paganism.

The other major change since 1970 dampening ecumenical optimism has been the emergence of non-denominational charismatic churches and networks, earlier described as a fifth surprise. Not only has this independent phenomenon been on an increasingly vast scale, it has brought a new divisiveness affecting not only the charismatic renewal but also the Pentecostal movement and even their own networks. The divisiveness has not just been a question of organizational independence, but for some has involved a radically different vision. Thus, particularly in the early years of the British House Church movement, some proponents of 'Church Restoration' rejected the possibility of the spiritual renewal of the mainline Churches.

## Signs of Hope

While the charismatic optimism of the 1970s is hardly possible today, there are significant signs of hope for Christian reconciliation within this over-all move of the Spirit. The imprint of the inter-church origins was sufficiently marked on many of the pioneers (e.g. Michael Harper, Larry Christenson, Kevin Ranaghan, Tom Forrest, Laurent Fabre) that the weakening in ecumenical expressions of renewal has been seen as a serious loss, threatening the vitality and authenticity of this whole work of God. From such convictions several inter-church charismatic bodies have been formed in the last decade: the North American

Renewal Service Committee, the European Charismatic Consultation and the International Charismatic Consultation on World Evangelization (that hosted the Brighton Congress of July 1991).

The Spirit of unity and reconciliation has also been blowing in other circles, often without much publicity. Within Youth with a Mission (YWAM), one of the largest para-church organizations, there has been a steady change in attitude towards co-operation with Catholics. Beginning in Europe in the late 1970s, this re-thinking was accepted by YWAM in 1984, when co-operation with the Catholic Church was approved as an acceptable option. In some countries, YWAM are now actively helping to form new Catholic faith communities.

Several centres of charismatic renewal have developed strong ministries of reconciliation, often in places of greatest social tension. Thus the Christian Renewal Centre, led by Anglican Cecil Kerr, at Rostrevor has worked for Catholic–Protestant reconciliation in Northern Ireland, and the Baptist Communauté de la Réconciliation, led by David Berly, in Lille, France, has done significant work for the homeless and has established close links with some black churches in South Africa. Charismatic congregations in South Africa are also known to have played a significant role in inter-racial reconciliation.

In recent years, there have also been encouraging signs of non-denominational leaders showing greater willingness to work with leaders in older Church traditions. Twenty years of experience have contributed to a greater humility, and a widespread recognition that the new churches face many of the same problems as the older church traditions. The administration for the Brighton Congress of July 1991 was handled by Terry Virgo's church in Hove, hub of one of the largest non-denominational networks in Britain. The Edinburgh City Fellowship led by Brian Hayes has developed significant relationships with the Catholic Church in Poland. Non-denominational leaders have also pioneered March for Jesus as a form of public witness open to all Christians.[1]

# A Test Issue

The question of unity is crucial for the Pentecostal and charismatic movements. This is not simply because these moves of the Spirit were trans-denominational in their origins, though that is important in demonstrating their essential reconciling mission. It is because unity is a test fruit of the Spirit. Only the Holy Spirit can fashion the unity of the body of Christ that transcends all distinctions and barriers of race, culture, gender, temperament and philosophy.

Whatever we may say about the justification of separation from Churches experienced as corrupt and oppressive[2], the spirit of divisiveness is always a sign of the adversary. A history of quarrels and divisions is a warning sign that a movement is not developing in accordance with God's plan. The unity–division rating is then a key indicator as to fidelity–infidelity. This thought should curb the folly of Pentecostal–charismatic triumphalism, and intensify the intercession of all those baptized in the Spirit.

# CHAPTER NINE

# THE NON-DENOMINATIONALS

At this point it is appropriate to examine more closely this new phenomenon of the 'non-denominational' charismatics, who in Britain have often been known as 'the House Churches'. It merits particular attention for several reasons: first, that while it does not fit into the pattern of original Pentecostal separation and subsequent charismatic acceptance, it is clearly occurring within the realm of Pentecostal–charismatic Christianity; secondly, it is happening world-wide on a scale that points to a particular significance within the wider movement.

## What is New in Non-Denominationalism

At first sight, it might seem that nothing is notably new in the phenomenon of charismatic independency. After all, much of the original Pentecostal movement involved the formation of independent assemblies and the spread of itinerant ministries acknowledging no churchly authority. Many Pentecostal denominations were initially formed by the association of local assemblies and ministers that exchanged the advantages of full independence for those of greater cohesion and organization. Even after the denominationalization of the Pentecostals movement, there were always independent evangelists and preachers, who were clearly Pentecostal by conviction and style. The number of independent Pentecostal increased again with the rise of the healing evangelists after World War II.

It is clear however that the new independent charismatics are not simply independent Pentecostals renamed in an age of charismatic renewal. The main thrust of charismatic non-denominationalism has not come from Pentecostal influences, but from milieux and concerns distinctively different in important respects from the Pentecostal Churches. The main exceptions are the 'prosperity gospel' networks, associated with Kenneth Hagin and Kenneth Copeland, often called 'Faith' or 'Rhema' churches, which in origin came out of a Pentecostal background that was never at ease with their teaching.

By contrast, the majority of the new independent charismatic churches and networks differ from the Pentecostals both in their social backgrounds and in their attitudes to the question of Church. First of all, the non-denominational leaders belong to the world of confident charismatic self-presentation, and have never known the struggle of the Pentecostal sub-culture to emerge from generations of isolation, both enforced and self-imposed. They are generally better-educated, move more easily in the modern world, and manifest fewer sectarian patterns of defensiveness and hostility. Quite a number have come from respectable Evangelical backgrounds, which had then rejected their charismatic testimony: particularly Plymouth Brethren in Britain and Southern Baptists in the United States.

Secondly, the majority of the non-denominationals represent a charismatic Christianity determined to overcome the weaknesses of much Protestant individualism. Both the U.S. origins in the Holy Spirit Teaching Mission in the late 1960s (later Christian Growth Ministries) and the British origins in the conferences convened a decade earlier by David Lillie and Arthur Wallis urged the importance of organic relationships in the body of Christ. While the American teaching on discipling was more pragmatic, the British emphasis was more doctrinal, picking up the traditional Brethren concern for the local manifestation of the Church. Even though the discipleship controversies of the 1970s have quieted down, there remains in the non-denominational groupings a concern for the Church and a conviction that this outpouring of the Spirit should lead to dynamic corporate expressions of spiritual life in the body of Christ.

Whereas the denominational charismatics have focused on the rediscovery of the spiritual gifts of 1 Corinthians 12:8–10, the non-denominational groupings have emphasized both the spiritual gifts of 1 Corinthians 12 and the ministry gifts of Ephesians 4:11 (apostle, prophet, evangelist, pastor–teacher). While a few Pentecostal groups tried to structure the ministry gifts, particularly the Apostolic Church in the first decades and the 'Latter Rain' movement out of Canada from the late 1940s, the non-denominationals in their determination not to become new denominations have generally managed to give scope for these ministries without institutionalizing them. We will need to return to the Ephesians 4:11 ministries when we consider the significance of these new independent streams.[1]

## Extent and Spread

Though the House Church movement in Britain is well-documented, it is a fast-moving phenomenon, and studies can become quickly outdated. In the 1980s, Andrew Walker's book *Restoring the Kingdom* examined the origins and development of the main streams of non-denominational charismatic revival in the British Isles. Even in the five years since Walker's revised edition, there have been significant new developments and forms of realignment. Among the major changes have been the continuing emergence of Terry Virgo (Hove, Sussex) and his New Frontiers network as a major force, and the disbanding of John Noble's Team Spirit (Romford, Essex) to reinforce the wider and looser Pioneer network led by Gerald Coates (Cobham, Surrey). While some groupings have not advanced, others progress. The Ichthus churches under Roger Forster's leadership have their major strength in the London area. The Jesus Fellowship (Bugbrooke, Northants), for years a vigorous and controversial force locally, is now establishing branches in many parts of the country. Most networks have a substantial outreach and programmes of church planting in other parts of the world. The vigour of these new churches is also evident from their contribution to Spring Harvest and to March for Jesus. March for Jesus, the public city-wide demonstrations of Christian faith now spreading to all continents, is a pan-Christian effort pioneered by three non-denominational leaders, Roger Forster and Graham Kendrick (Ichthus) and Gerald Coates, together with Lynn Green (YWAM).

In the United States, there are innumerable independent charismatic congregations, many of them called 'covenant' or 'community' churches. The links between the U.S. independent churches are generally looser than in Britain, though there are some closer networks, like the People of Destiny (centred in Gaithersburg, Maryland) with a pattern of an overall apostolic team.[2] The emerging American pattern seems to be one of the more influential pastors and larger churches offering a wide variety of services to other pastors without requiring explicit forms of commitment. This obviously shows the influence of entrepreneurial business practices within the sphere of Christian ministry. Among the new non-denominational groupings of American origin, now found in many countries, are the Vineyard Fellowships, associated with John Wimber (Anaheim, California) now numbering 274 local assemblies. David Barrett's statistics for North America show that independent charismatics account for more than double the number of denominational charismatics (nearly 14 million compared to 6 million).

In several other parts of the world, there has also been an explosion of new independent charismatic churches. Thailand, traditionally a difficult country for Christian missionaries, has seen a remarkable network of churches develop under the leadership of Kriengsak Chareonwongsak, pastor of the Hope of Bangkok Church. East Asia has also seen other remarkable growth of independent charismatic churches, particularly in Indonesia and the Philippines.

## Their Significance

However great their challenge and affront to the older Churches, not only to the Catholic Church and to the

Churches of the Reformation, but also to the Pentecostals, it is important to recognize that the new independent charismatic churches are part of the wider Pentecostal–charismatic phenomenon. They also arose from Christians being baptized in the Spirit, and manifesting the same gifts and endowments of the Spirit as the Pentecostals and the denominational charismatics. Their worship is unquestionably charismatic in style and power, and their musicians, especially Graham Kendrick, have contributed significantly to the new songs used across the whole movement. The books and tapes of their leaders are recognized and sold in the wider streams of charismatic renewal.

The majority of the new independent charismatic assemblies and networks clearly affirm the central truths of Christian faith: the Trinity, the divinity and humanity of Christ, his virgin birth and his resurrection from the dead, the redemption through the blood of the cross, justification by faith, the outpouring of the Spirit at Pentecost, the necessity of repentance for sin, the second coming of Christ.[3] For those in the mainline Churches concerned about the real dangers exposed by such tragedies as Jonestown in Guyana and Waco, Texas, the following considerations are relevant:

(a) Most of the independent charismatic assemblies, at least in Europe and North America, do not manifest the exclusive isolationist patterns of the fringe groups totally dominated by so-called 'charismatic' personalities. They value fellowship among leaders; hence the importance of the networks, which they are determined not to allow to become fixed institutions.

(b) They place a high value on basic Christian orthodoxy. Indeed, many people have joined the non-denominational ranks because of deviant teaching and lack of orthodoxy in the Churches they left.[4]

(c) They are as aware as anyone else of the dangers of doctrinal deviation, and may in fact be more aggressive in their opposition to 'semi-Christian' cults that cloak aberrant beliefs in Christian terms.

(d) Undoubtedly, leadership in the independent

sector has been stronger and more assertive than the patterns now found in many of the older Churches, and this factor has a bearing on their impact and success. A fair judgment might be that their temptations are different. The older Churches often lack strong and courageous leadership, though it is not hard to think of notable exceptions, and the pressures to compromise the Spirit's work are greater. The newer Churches more frequently run the risk of strong leadership turning into authoritarianism and of personality clashes producing further fragmentation.

It is important to recognize that the non-denominationals belong to the wider Pentecostal–charismatic movement against opposed tendencies to deny it. On the one hand, some people within the mainline Church traditions easily see the non-denominational sector as intrinsically an aberration, as yet another example of a divisive sectarianism that is simply to be deplored. This attitude is more common among Catholics, though happily it is not prevalent in Catholic charismatic circles in English-speaking countries.

On the other hand, the independent groupings can be tempted to deny that they are part of the wider charismatic movement, particularly through a dogmatic rejection of the mainline Churches as apostate and unrenewable. Some years ago, a prominent British House Church leader, Arthur Wallis, argued that they belonged to a Restoration movement that was both independent of and prior to the charismatic renewal. This historical reinterpretation misunderstands the distinctiveness of the Pentecostal–charismatic movement, centred on baptism in the Spirit, and gives a priority to a movement current based on a particular doctrinal emphasis, the theology of the Church coming from an antecedent tradition (the Brethren). This is in principle no different from any other denial of the over-all identity of the Pentecostal and charismatic movement on the grounds of doctrinal differences.

The over-all significance of the non-denominational charismatics must then be sought within the framework of the one movement of Pentecostal–charismatic blessing and its place in Christian history. What is most significant has to be what has contributed to their astonishing rate of growth, even in a movement known for its spiritual dynamism.

The new charismatic churches are typically oriented to church growth and expansion. Not being renewal groups within existing church allegiances, their focus is not on renewal of existing bodies, but on planting new churches. It is here that their acceptance of the Ephesians 4:11 ministries and their non-denominationalism both play a significant role.

Not being new denominations by structure, the independent networks do not have any received patterns of ministry or ministerial training. While they have no status difference between an ordained clergy and an unordained laity, they have many full-time workers. The Ephesians 4:11 ministries are more outward and mission-oriented, particularly those of apostle and evangelist, than the ministry structures of the mainline Churches, at least in their present form. The astonishing growth-rate of the independent churches is then the direct result of dynamic charismatic faith issuing in structures and deployment of resources directly geared to evangelism and church planting. In this, the non-denominationals are aided by their organizational flexibility, and the more immediate availability of their resources for missionary and pastoral work. Their greater freedom from sectarian mentalities and their confident modernity have given them significant evangelistic and strategic advantages over many Pentecostal initiatives, at least in Europe and North America.

## The Paradox

On the one hand, there is clear evidence of the Pentecostal–charismatic outpouring of the Spirit in the twentieth century having a unitive purpose. This purpose is particularly manifest in the series of surprises of the Spirit outlined in Chapter Two. On the other hand, the most dynamic growth worldwide in the last decade has been in the independent or non-denominational sector (and in many parts of the Third World among the Pentecostals)[6]. This expansion has increased tensions between the new churches and the older-established Christian Churches and missionary agencies.

At this point, it is only possible to hold this paradox within a framework of faith, hope and love. That is to insist that both the non-denominational explosion and the unitive thrust of the Spirit in the sequence of divine surprises are fundamentally works of the Holy Spirit, even though we cannot yet see how they fit together. Maintaining this paradox will mean resisting the temptation to find the full meaning of God's renewing-restoring purpose in one to the exclusion of the other. Both the charismatic renewal in the mainline Churches and the non-denominational explosion bear the hall-marks of significant works of the Lord.

Because all streams, including the non-denominationals, stem from baptism in the Spirit, there is a real kinship of the Spirit between them. There is more co-operation and fellowship between denominational and non-denominational charismatics than the tensions and occasional polemics would suggest. Otherwise it would be impossible for prominent charismatic magazines such as *Renewal* in Britain and *Charisma* in the USA to cover and serve both these sectors.

We turn now to examine the nature of this unity flowing from baptism in the Spirit. Only as the character of this new-found unity in the Spirit is identified will it be possible to see how it differs from full sacramental ecclesial communion and how it can contribute to the organic unity of reconciled Churches.

# CHAPTER TEN

# UNITY IN THE HEAVENLIES

Both the wonder and the fragility of the newly-given unity among the Spirit-baptized make it imperative that we understand the nature of this unity given in and through baptism in the Spirit, and how this spiritual unity relates to doctrinal, pastoral and governmental unity in the Church. The clue to this relationship lies in the heavenly character of the life in the Spirit.

As noted in Chapter Five, Christians baptized in the Spirit have been opened up to experience the heavenly character of the Christian life. As a result, they have a basis in their experience for knowing that their inheritance is imperishable, stored up in heaven (1 Pet 1:4). They are living on earth, but their citizenship is in heaven (Phil 3:20). As an element in lived experience, this heavenly dimension can now become a conscious element in their motivation.

## Raised to the Heavenlies

The Pauline letters do not merely assert the reception of a heavenly gift on earth. Paul reflects that those 'baptized into [Christ's] death' (Rom 6:3) are established in Christ, who is himself established in heaven at the right hand of the Father. Because we are even now in him, in some sense we must already be where he is. So he writes: 'Your life is hid with Christ in God' (Col 3:3).

This thought is carried further in the letter to the Ephesians: 'Blessed be the God and Father of our Lord Jesus Christ, who has blessed us in Christ with every spiritual blessing in the heavenly places' (Eph 1:3). This statement expresses God's eternal purpose, the mind of the Creator from all eternity. This promise enters the life of the believer when the Christian hears 'the word of truth', believes in Christ and is 'sealed with the promised Holy Spirit' (Eph 1:13).

A connection is then made between 'the immeasurable greatness of his power in us who believe' (1:19) and 'the working of his great might' accomplished in the resurrection of Christ (1:19–20). The unlimited power of the Spirit, most powerfully demonstrated in the resurrection, is first manifested in the Christian by the gift of the Spirit which creates a heavenly risen life within the believer. The next step in the argument is that God has 'raised us up with him, and made us sit with him in the heavenly places in Christ Jesus' (Eph 2:6).

The Christian's establishment in the heavenlies is the consequence of Christ's ascension. The Christian's heavenly position is hidden until the Parousia, when all will be gloriously manifested, and the polarity between heaven and earth will be ended: 'For you have died, and your life is hid with Christ in God. When Christ who is our life appears, then you also will appear with him in glory' (Col 3:3–4).

## Consequences for Christian Unity

This heavenly character revealed in the Spirit-filled life has important repercussions for Christian fellowship, for our understanding of the Church and for Christian unity. The whole Christian life brought about by the Spirit of God has both an earthly and a heavenly character. Our lives are lived on earth, and on earth we are brought into the visible fellowship of the Church. But the new reality of the Christian fellowship, the Church, cannot be confined to the earth. Our head, Christ, is in heavenly glory, and we are included in him. He is made present on earth so that we can be made present in heaven.

The unity of the Church is supremely in heaven, because it is the unity of Christ and those inserted into his life. This truth is expressed in all the eucharistic liturgies in which the worshippers on earth join with the angels and saints in their heavenly hymn of praise 'Holy, holy, holy is the Lord of hosts' (Isa 6:3).

The unity of the Church is not first of all something put together on earth, even though effected by the power of the Holy Spirit. It is established in heaven because it is totally founded in the ascended Christ. In heaven, this unity is not partial. We are not totally in heaven, but the unity in heaven is total. In this life we are in the world but not of the world (John 17:11,16); we are still on earth where our unity with one another in Christ is impaired.

Thus often Christians can think in relation to other Churches (e.g. Catholics vis-à-vis Orthodox, Lutherans, Anglicans; Baptists vis-à-vis Pentecostals etc.) that we are 70 per cent united but 30 per cent divided; or 60 per cent achieved and 40 per cent to go. The work of ecumenical reconciliation then aims to raise the united percentage and lower the divided. But understanding the heavenly dimension of the Christian life shows that we are 100 per cent united in heaven, and the united/divided percentages only apply on earth. In this perspective, the ecumenical task is to realize the existing heavenly unity more and more on earth: 'Thy will be done on earth as *it is in heaven*'.

## An Anticipation of the Unity of Heaven

This spiritual unity in the heavenlies is given in anticipation of the unity of the glorified body of Christ at his return. It is like an advance aura cast by the coming event of the Parousia. It is lived by faith in the promise. This faith is like that of the patriarchs who 'all died in faith, not having received what was promised, but having seen it and greeted it from afar' (Heb 11:13). In the new covenant, however, the Christian does not only greet the promise from afar, but already in the gift of the Spirit has an initial taste of the reality promised.

When charismatic Christians have fellowship in the Spirit with charismatic Christians in other Churches and streams, they begin to have a shared awareness of their unity in the heavenlies. This unity is sometimes dismissed as mere emotional exuberance. However, its genuinely spiritual character is shown by the ability of charismatic Christians from different backgrounds to worship together in the Spirit, to share their witness, to recognize the same Spirit in each other, to engage in common evangelism. These would not be possible if the common element was only shared emotion.

In the charismatic renewal, ecumenical sharing not thought possible before has sprung up spontaneously, ahead of our confessional theology. This is most obvious in the spread of joint evangelism and ecumenical communities. This sharing in evangelism and in community living between Catholics and Protestants can only survive when it is rooted both in shared faith about the Christ-event in the past and in shared faith about the Christ-coming in the future. They can live with the real differences that remain because they have a faith-grasp on the eternal reality that unites them and draws them forward to itself. They are together hidden with Christ in God, and their new earthly fellowship manifests something of this hidden unity. Their sharing is a sign of hope for the Churches, that the coming Lord is more powerful than the enemy who sows the tares of division. It proclaims in deed that what unites is more fundamental than what divides.

This heavenly unity in the Spirit has to be translated into earthly unity in heart, mind and will. To argue from invisible spiritual unity against the need for organic Church unity is to misunderstand the nature of the Church and the relationship between the heavenly and the earthly. If divided Christians who have discovered a new depth of unity in the Spirit do not work to translate their spiritual unity into earthly embodiment, they will find this spiritual unity imperilled. It is a condition of having the heavenly life that we seek to conform our whole lives and communities to the divine gift. This is the permeating of our whole souls, our minds and our wills, that is our cherished patterns of thinking and our affections, as well as our theology, our worship and our service, with the life of the outpoured Spirit.

Understanding the heavenly character of the gift of the Spirit enables us to explain how the experienced unity of those baptized in the Spirit is not merely emotional, but truly spiritual. Explaining the relationship between the spiritual and the rest of our human make-up shows how our hold on this spiritual unity is necessarily fragile until it is translated into the unity of the whole person and of the whole fellowship of persons in the visible organic Church on earth.

This elevation to the heavenlies in accordance with the eternal plan of God has to ground any deep appropriation of the grace of baptism in the Spirit. The outpouring of the Spirit is not simply concerned with healing what is sick and deformed and with empowering what is weak, but brings nearer the full realization of God's purpose 'hidden for ages and generations but now made manifest to his saints' (Col 1:26).

# CHAPTER ELEVEN

# AN UNKNOWN PIONEER

In this chapter, we will make a brief detour, and look at the relevance for understanding the Pentecostal and charismatic movements of the life and thought of a man who remains largely unknown outside the limited circles in which he moved.

Louis Dallière, a pastor of the French Reformed Church, was born in Chicago in 1897, the son of an English Anglican mother and a French Catholic father. After his basic training for the Reformed ministry, Dallière studied the American philosopher W. E. Hocking for a year at Yale. After further studies in France, he began in 1925 his lengthy pastorate at Charmes-sur-Rhône, a village in the Ardèche region on the west bank of the Rhône between Lyon and Avignon. His importance for our topic lies in the events of 1930–32, which set his life in a new direction.

Years of seeking for a deeper life in the Spirit were crowned in 1930 with an experience of the Lord that Dallière always called his baptism in the Spirit. Subsequently, through the ministry of Douglas Scott, an Elim Pentecostal evangelist from London, Dallière received the gift of tongues and discovered the Pentecostal revival as the answer to his prayers. In complete contrast to this self-taught evangelist, Dallière was knowledgeable in theology and Church history. During his spiritual search, he had reflected much on the Evangelical revivals in Protestantism, and immediately sensed the major significance of this gift of 'Pentecost'. Zealous student that he was, Dallière spent two weeks in Britain in the summer of 1932 studying the Pentecostal revival through George Jeffreys and the Elim movement. His reflections were published the same year in a small book entitled *D'Aplomb sur la Parole de Dieu* (literally 'Squarely on the Word of God').

There is a depth in Dallière's reflections even at this early stage of his pentecostal experience. They show a remarkable clarity of spiritual thinking; from the beginning he is thinking with God, begging the light of the Holy Spirit upon his experience. He raises his gaze to the full scope of God's work, with a focus not limited to his own Church:

> If today God should give anew a spiritual communion with himself, accompanied by speaking in tongues, it would be a grace so marvellous for us, that there would be every reason, not to scorn this gift, but to praise and glorify the name of the Lord. The whole question is to know if the facts are exact and if they are of God.[1]

From the start of his pentecostal experience, Dallière was convinced that this grace was for the revival and renewal of the Church. In 1932 he went to a Pentecostal convention at Le Havre and met a young missionary from Wales, Thomas Roberts, to whom he confided that the Lord had forbidden him to leave the Reformed Church, a conviction that others among his new Pentecostal friends would find difficult to accept. In his assiduous reading of church history, Dallière saw a sharp contrast between true revivals and sects. While revivals are of the Church and for the Church, sects are outside the Church and against the Church. Whereas revivals highlight the fundamental doctrines of the Church, sects organize around special points of doctrine. In studying this new movement of Pentecost, he took as a criterion of discernment whether it was a true revival of the Church or whether it was inherently sectarian. From the following passage we can sense the reverence and gravity with which Dallière approached this strange phenomenon:

At the beginning of Darbyism [the Plymouth Brethren] there was a man, Darby; at the beginning of the revival we are studying there was . . . a Pentecost. The religious facts and realities here precede the doctrines, as in all the great movements of Christian awakening. When we think that these religious realities have been manifested, without the intervention of any teacher or founder of a sect, at points as scattered on the globe as California and India, we have to set aside any idea that we are dealing with phenomena of collective emotions. It seems that a much higher influence is at work: that of God himself or the other one! Again we are faced with the same question as before: are these happenings authentic, are they of God?[2]

During World War II, when travel was very difficult in France, Dallière continued to study the Word and pray about this outpouring of the Spirit. His vision became clearer in these years, and found expression in the charter of the Union de Prière, a kind of sodality or guild within the Reformed Church, that Dallière founded in 1946. It proposed four major topics for the daily prayer of the members:

(1)  The Revival of Churches through the Conversion of Souls.
(2)  The Salvation of the Jewish People.
(3)  The Visible Unity of the Body of Christ.
(4)  The Coming of Jesus Christ and the Resurrection of the Dead.

Dallière was convinced that these four points expressed the heart of God poured out in this baptism in the Spirit. Before the charismatic renewal had appeared, this Reformed theologian had grasped in prayer the true scope of this twentieth-century outpouring of the Spirit of God.

What is truly astonishing is that Dallière was developing this vision at a time when it appeared less and less likely to be realized. For while he remained within the French Reformed Church to witness there to this pentecostal grace, the Pentecostals were becoming more denominationalized and closed to the working of the Spirit in the mainline Churches. Only Thomas Roberts from the Pentecostal side resonated with Dallière's spirit.

Even though this revival only touched a limited circle within the French Reformed Church, Dallière knew that it was meant for all the Churches. So he wrote to the astonished Thomas Roberts: 'Every separated Church, including the Catholic Church, as well as the Lutheran and the Reformed, and all the Free Churches, will be purified and will enter into the body of the Bridegroom.' Dallière was much exercised in his spirit about what he termed the 'duality' between the Churches and the movements of revival. He longed for the renewal and revival of the Church, and he grieved over this partial dichotomy between his Church and the currents of new life from the Spirit.

From the time of his baptism in the Spirit the unifying theme in Dallière's writing and ministry was corporate preparation for the return of the Lord. In 1932, the eschatological convictions of the Elim Pentecostals in Britain made an obvious impression: 'Thus they explain that the supernatural graces so indispensable at the beginning have become so once again because it is the end.'[3] But Dallière with his greater ecclesial sense realized that the Church is called to prepare corporately for the return of her Lord and Bridegroom. This was the framework in which he saw the outpouring of the Spirit. This was the context in which he approached the divisions among Christians, the summons to unity and the calling of the Jewish people. Even before the creation of the state of Israel in 1948, Dallière was being taught by the Spirit concerning the Lord's own people.

Louis Dallière was convinced of the necessity of repentance in relation to each of the four prayer intentions. Repentance is needed for revival and the conversion of souls; repentance is needed on all sides for these conversions to lead to Church revival. Gentile Christians must repent for the sins of the (Gentile) Church against the Jews; each Church must repent for its sins against the unity of the body of Christ. Christians must repent for their lack of desire for the Parousia.

All four topics are closely linked. There is an inner logic binding them together. Revival has to be of the Church and for the upbuilding of the Church. The charter of the Union de Prière affirms: 'Prayer for unity is bound up with prayer for the illumination of the Jewish people' (para. 38). The Church was most united, the charter states, when the Churches of the Gentiles were 'imitators of the churches of God in Christ Jesus which are in Judea' (1 Thess 2:14). The section of the charter on Christian unity ends with the striking statement:

> The Union senses that it will be the converted Jewish people who will restore to the Church its visible unity. What the younger son of the parable has not been able to do, despite all his love for the Christ, the older brother will help him to accomplish – we do not know where or how – when, restored to the banquet room of his Father, they will prepare together 'the church ... holy and without blemish' (Eph 5:27), that will be presented to the Lord on his return. (para 48)

Dallière saw a close link between Israel and the second coming. It was not only that the Jewish people would turn to Jesus before his return, but also that Jewish understanding of body and spirit, of earth and heaven, formed a bulwark against the two Gentile tendencies to be too much at home in this world and then to posit a wrongly-spiritualized heaven after death: 'In general, Gentile Christianity has always preferred that Christ should not come again: life on this earth, more or less Christianized, appeared sufficient, with its prolongation in the beatitude of the soul separated in death from the body' (*Charter*, para. 58).

Dallière saw the prayer for the second coming as essentially linked with prayer for the final conquest of death.

It is necessary to desire victory over death: for this, one must desire that Jesus return in glory, in accordance with the prophecies of the new covenant, as he came in humility in the womb of the Virgin Mary in accordance with the prophecies of the old covenant. (*Charter*, para. 61)

The Union de Prière did not take up a position regarding the millennium, leaving this free to the biblical interpretation of its members. It focused not on what we might call the mechanics of eschatology, but on the core of the Christian hope:

what matters is that the era of the Holy Spirit, or the time of the end, has been opened on the day of Pentecost; that we continue to live this grace; and that it will be fulfilled one day when all things will be placed in the hands of Jesus Christ for the Resurrection and the Judgment.' (*Charter*, para. 64)[4]

# PART II

## Principles

# CHAPTER TWELVE

# THE NEW AND THE OLD

T he outpouring of the Spirit in a sovereign move of God forcibly confronts all Christians with the issue of the new and the old. The popularity among Pentecostals and charismatics of the words of Jesus that new wine requires new wineskins (Matt 9:17) illustrates this challenge. It was this perennial issue of the new and the old in the realm of Christ and the Spirit that had so occupied the mind of Louis Dallière.

The tensions between the new and the old are constantly manifested in these movements:

- spontaneous free worship versus received liturgical forms
- new churches versus revitalization of old Churches
- new capacities of the spirit versus elevation of natural faculties
- new teachings versus received doctrine
- new ministries versus historic patterns.

## New Life for the Christian

The Holy Spirit brings new life in Christ. Pentecostal–charismatic language witnesses to newness: new life, new power, new hope, new gifts. This newness is evidenced in the New Testament, especially in the new life as a share in the resurrection of Jesus. The life of the Spirit is new, because it involves a death to the old life-principle, and *birth* to a new. In this way, the New Testament makes clear that the Christian life is not just an improvement or a revamping of existing life, but is truly a resurrection from the dead.

Thus, the sense that the gift of the Spirit involves the beginning of something truly new is correct. It expresses the truth of *regeneration*, of God bringing something to life, of divine interventions that create new life. This is at the level of *spirit*. In regeneration through the word of truth and the bath of baptism, the Christian receives new life from God. This is the heavenly gift, emphasized in Chapter Ten. What comes sovereignly from heaven has to have a radical newness. We see this in the Pentecost events of Jerusalem and Caesarea; we see it in the conversion of Saul of Tarsus; we see it in the visions of John of Patmos.

As a result of this gift of new life, the Christian can exercise new capacities not previously operative. These include the power to praise God, to hear the Lord, to pray in the name of Jesus. The new life is not just something invisible, hidden within the believer; it is an active dynamic power, seeking embodiment in the total life and personality of the recipient.

However, what is poured out sovereignly from the throne of God comes into what has to be renewed; it comes into history, it comes into the Church, it comes into existing human lives. This new life of the Spirit is poured into what already exists and becomes its principle of renewal. So as well as the pattern of regeneration, there is the framework of conversion. Conversion means a complete change of direction of what already exists (it is captured in two word roots used in the New Testament: *epistrephein*, to turn around, and *metanoia*, change of mind or heart). Everything already operative in the person has to be converted. In origin all this comes from the hand of God in creation, and is thus in its essential nature good (Gen 1 *passim*). But through sin it has become distorted, fragmented and frustrated. Thus the process of conversion is also a healing of what is deeply wounded[1]. So there is both a new creation of the spirit and a conversion–healing of the existing person with all the faculties of soul, of mind, will and memory being brought under the sway of the new life.

Newness and freshness then always characterize God's acts of pouring out his Spirit of new life. It is in the most holy Christians, those whom many Christians call the saints, that the distinctive personality of each is most fully seen. In God's kingdom, there are no clones. Each holy person shows forth to the world a uniqueness never seen before: yes, the holiness they reveal is the same, the Lord manifested is the same, the power that produces it is the same, but the resulting portrait is always a new masterpiece of divine grace.

The complementarity of regeneration and conversion provides one model for understanding the relationship between the new and the old in the work of the Spirit. Against those who are congenitally suspicious of the new, especially in matters of religion, it is necessary to emphasize that there is a truly new and totally creative act of God in regeneration and every coming of the Holy Spirit. On the other hand, it is important to show the enthusiasts for novelty that the old is not abolished. There is something to be renewed: a person, a society, a culture, even the Church.

## Continuity and Discontinuity

The new and the old in Christian life are closely related to the issues of continuity and discontinuity in the life of the Church. The new represents the element of discontinuity, of the sovereign irruption of the unexpected and the unplanned in Christian history. The new expresses what was not and now is. The old represents the element of continuity, of that which does not come and go, but perdures and develops. The old is embodied in structures and institutions, rituals and creeds. It corresponds to the element of *transmission* of life, symbolized in the biblical genealogies and the role of Mary in the Incarnation.

The continuity–discontinuity relationship is grounded in the make-up of the human, that is, in persons developing in society. While the spirit expresses communion with the eternal in heaven, the body is the vehicle of continuity on earth. While the spirit expresses individual personality, the body grounds the identity of the species and the possibility of society. Thus it is only as spiritual impulses become embodied that they acquire a social context and a history. 'The Word became flesh and dwelt among us' (John 1:14). Jesus is conceived by the Spirit (heavenly-vertical) but born of Mary (earthly-horizontal).

Thus there is an essential interaction between the new and the old, the continuous and the discontinuous. Each contributes a necessary element to the life of the historical and growing Christian community. Exalting one and dismissing the other is a sure recipe for imbalance with all its ensuing problems.

## New Life for the Church

However, it is not only at the level of individuals that the outpouring of the Spirit brings new life. There is something authentically new in every corporate work of the Spirit of God. This is again a consequence of the nature of the Holy Spirit and of sovereign irruptions of grace in human history.

No movement of the Spirit in the history of the Church is ever simply a repetition of an earlier pattern. There have been many movements of the Spirit of God in Christian history: the monastic movement of the third and fourth centuries; the Celtic missionary movements of the sixth to eighth centuries; the monastic reform of the eleventh and twelfth centuries; the mendicant movements of evangelical simplicity in the twelfth and thirteenth centuries; the Hesychast movement in Greek Orthodoxy; the Carmelite reform associated with St Teresa of Avila and St John of the Cross; the French spiritual school of the seventeenth century; the Pietist and Moravian movements in seventeenth and eighteenth-century German Protestantism; the Wesleyan movement in eighteenth-century Britain and the Great Awakening in North America; the nineteenth-century Haugean revival in Norwegian Lutheranism; the Welsh Revivals of 1859 and 1904;

the East African Revival from the 1930s. Each has its distinctive character. None is perfect in its final results. But all were perfect in the impulses that came from the Spirit. And what the Spirit produced was a marvellous variety, all revealing the Lord Jesus, all flowing from his cross and resurrection, all manifesting faith, hope and love. But the way in which they did so was new in every instance: a new face radiating the one and ancient love. Authentic movements of the Spirit of God are never just restorations of the past, never simply attempts to restore some imagined golden age.

The irruption of the Spirit in the Pentecostal and charismatic movements has given rise to many practices, experiences and phenomena that have a quality of newness. This does not mean that they have no historical precedents, which is evidently untrue. However, they do represent a distinctive form of making present and operative specific gifts and graces previously known in different patterns. They also reach us as things outside our previous horizons of experience and expectation. Knowledge of historical precedents never equips anyone to predict contemporary manifestations of the Spirit. For example, there are various historical instances of speaking in tongues or similar practices like Richard Rolle's interior song in the fourteenth century and the earlier phenomenon of *jubilatio* of which St Augustine of Hippo wrote. But none anticipate exactly either the patterns of glossolalia associated with baptism in the Spirit or the congregational harmonization of tongues that is a regular feature of Pentecostal–charismatic worship.

Similarly, it would seem that simultaneous congregational praise represents something never previously known in exactly this form. Yes, people have raised their arms in worship before. Indeed, it was commended in the first letter to Timothy (2:8); mosaics in the Roman catacombs depict Christians praying with uplifted arms. Surely too the Church did not have to wait for the Pentecostals before Christians made 'a joyful noise unto the Lord' (Ps 95:2; 98:4; 100:1). No doubt too but that American revivalist patterns and Afro-American forms

of expression made their contribution. But the precise
forms of bodily and vocal expression that characterize
Pentecostal–charismatic worship would seem to be a
fresh creation of the Spirit, drawing from the divine
treasury things new and old: new in their expression,
old in their inner life and significance.

The most obviously new features in Pentecostal–charismatic life are perhaps the diverse forms of ministry that
are not provided for in the inherited structures of any of
the major Christian traditions, whether the older three-
fold ministry of bishop, priest and deacon, or subsequent
patterns of Presbyterian, Congregationalist or Quaker
traditions. For some, the evident novelty and resulting
incongruity with received tradition form an argument,
at least for caution, and maybe for rejection. However,
the mainline Churches do not seem to have accorded
enough weight to the truly creative work of the Holy
Spirit. In such a perspective, it is not inappropriate that
such an outpouring of the Spirit should raise up gifts and
endowments that are not easily received into existing
patterns. The difficulty of integration then reflects the
extent of the Spirit's challenge.

Another aspect of the creativity of the Spirit in the
charismatic movement is the rise of new types of Christian community. Unlike the spiritual gifts, community
life has a long Christian history reflecting great variety:
the apostolic community in Jerusalem; the monastic communities following the rules of Basil and Benedict; the
Canons Regular of the twelfth century; the friars of the
thirteenth; the Paraguayan reductions of the seventeenth
century; the Moravian Brethren at Herrnhut, Germany
in the eighteenth century; on a smaller scale the restoration of the Hutterites in the twentieth century. The
covenant communities springing up within the charismatic renewal reflect a new pattern of corporate life
that includes whole families and is less dependent on
large buildings, in a way adapted to a mobile and largely
urban society. Again the genre is old, but the particular
form is authentically new.

However, the new is never created without a context,

and is always linked to the renewal of the old. That is to say, there is a parallel between regeneration and conversion in the individual Christian, and the birth of new forms and the renewal of the old in the corporate setting of the Church. However there is one major difference: for the Christian, regeneration is the beginning; but for the Church, this outpouring of the Spirit is not a beginning, but a new grace in a long history of unfailing divine mercy and mixed human response.

Here the dialectic of the new and the old can help us to formulate what is perhaps the biggest challenge posed by an ecumenical grace of the Spirit, a challenge that confronts Catholics and new denominations in opposed ways. For the Catholics and others upholding apostolic succession, the issue is: how can the grace of Pentecost, which is for the Church, appear and flourish outside the apostolic succession? For Pentecostals and non-denominationals, the challenge is: how can any new grace in Christian history not have an essential link with the historic embodiments of the new covenant?

We need then to probe the Scriptures to learn more about the new and the old, about the differences between the creativity of the Spirit and the mere novelties of restless humans. We need to understand more about God's promises and how God deals with the infidelity of those to whom the promises had been given. The following chapters seek to uncover these principles before applying them to the Pentecostal and charismatic movements.

# CHAPTER THIRTEEN

# THE PARTICULAR IN VIEW OF THE WHOLE

The first principle concerning interventions of the Lord in human history is: *God always acts towards the particular in view of the whole*. That is to say, God never acts except in relation to God's total plan and purpose.

God always has the end in view from the beginning. Thus the Lord spoke to the prophet 'declaring the end from the beginning and from ancient times things not yet done, saying, "My counsel shall stand, and I will accomplish all my purpose"' (Isa 46:10). In the divine mind, all is one, and all details have their place in relation to God's over-all purpose in creation. It is a weakness and limitation of human behaviour to act for short-term goals while forgetting the long-term implications. God always acts eternally for eternal purposes.

Forgetting this principle leads to God's chosen adopting élitist postures and making exclusive claims. For Pentecostal and charismatic Christians, it can lead to dismissal of other Christian groups as irrelevant, part of the débris left behind by the onward sweep of the Spirit. It is a constant temptation of those who experience the blessing of God in tangible ways to imagine that these graces are given primarily for their own benefit. This danger may be all the greater among Christians without a sense of history and tradition.

## Israel as a Priestly People

The principle that particular people are chosen for the sake of all is clearly shown in the call of Israel. From

Israel's origins in the call of Abraham, it is promised that through him 'all the families of the earth shall be blessed' (Gen 12:3). By calling Abraham 'from the nations' God will fashion a people for himself who will become the instrument of God's blessing for all the nations (see also Gen 22:18). Israel is in origin a people in contrast to the nations (the *goyim*, the Gentiles). They are not in origin a nation among nations, but a people set apart as the bearers of salvation for all the nations.

The promise is to those who follow in the faith of Abraham. The grounds for the promise are the faithfulness of God to his word. 'God is not man, that he should lie, or a son of man, that he should repent. Has he said, and will he not do it? Or has he spoken, and will he not fulfil it?' (Num 23:19).

To represent all peoples before God is to be a priestly people. 'Now therefore, if you will obey my voice and keep my covenant, you shall be my own possession among all peoples; for all the earth is mine, and you shall be to me a kingdom of priests and a holy nation' (Exod 19:5–6). As a people or kingdom, Israel is priestly of its nature, chosen to minister to the whole creation.

The universal scope of God's saving purpose reappears strongly in the exilic and post-exilic prophets. The agony of the exile in Babylon brought the Jews face to face with the reason for their separate existence. In the first suffering servant song of Isaiah, we read: 'I am the Lord, I have called you in righteousness, I have taken you by the hand and kept you; I have given you as a covenant to the people, a light to the nations' (Isa 42:6).

The particular call of Israel is intensified in the call of Jerusalem, the holy city. Jerusalem, which becomes the focal point of Israel, will also be the instrument of God's blessings for all humanity: 'These [foreigners] I will bring to my holy mountain, and make them joyful in my house of prayer; their burnt offerings and their sacrifices will be accepted on my altar; for my house shall be called a house of prayer for all peoples' (Isa 56:7).

The blessing of the nations will depend on Israel's fidelity to her priestly call.

'If you return, O Israel, says the Lord, to me you should return. If you remove your abominations from my presence, and do not waver, and if you swear, "As the Lord lives," in truth, in justice, and in uprightness, then nations shall bless themselves in him, and in him shall they glory.' (Jer 4:1–2)

This fidelity to her priestly vocation for the sake of all reaches its fulfilment in Jesus himself, the embodiment of Israel (cf. Isa 49:3, 5–6), who as great high priest will offer his life for the ransom of all humanity.

## The Church a Priestly People

In the same way, the Christian Church is called for the sake of all peoples, not just for the sake of its present membership. Peter takes up the teaching from Exodus concerning the nature of the covenant people: 'But you are a chosen race, a royal priesthood, a holy nation, God's own people, that you may declare the wonderful deeds of him who called you out of darkness into his marvellous light' (1 Pet 2:9). The 'chosen race' is also a 'royal priesthood', that is, they are chosen for the others whom they will serve as priests. This passage indicates the priestly character of evangelism, the declaration of God's wonderful deeds to those who do not know them (see Rom 15:16).

The Christian Church is based on the call of the one man, Jesus Christ, who truly represents all, dies for all, and is raised for all. Through his resurrection and the gift of the Spirit, Jesus becomes the head of a body. Every move of the Spirit is related both to Jesus and to his body, the Church.

Similarly, any Christian call is for the sake of the whole Church, and through the Church for the whole race. Saul of Tarsus is chosen to be 'a chosen instrument . . . to carry [God's] name before the Gentiles and kings and the sons of Israel' (Acts 9:15). Writing of ministries and gifts within the body of Christ, Paul says: 'To *each* is given the manifestation of the Spirit for *the common good*' (1 Cor 12:7 italics mine).

So, in the history of the Church, God raises up people and groups to play particular roles in the divine plan. But these calls always serve God's purpose for the Church. We find this in Francis of Assisi and the Franciscan movement, in Gerard Groote and the Brethren of the Common Life, in Count Zinzendorf and the Moravian Brethren, in John Wesley and the Methodist Societies, in Teresa of Avila and the Carmelite Reform.

This principle even applies to movements like the Anabaptists that evidenced both the presence of the Holy Spirit and a separatist mentality, urging all true believers to 'come ye out from among them'. The separate existence of a Christian tradition can still represent a grace and a word of the Lord for all, even if its contribution to the wider Church is not realized for centuries. It is the task and grace of the call to Christian unity to draw out and to realize this 'gift-for-all' potential.

In this light, the Pentecostal and charismatic movements centred on baptism in the Spirit are to be understood as gifts of God (a) to the whole body of Christ and (b) for the sake of the whole world. They are not a replacement Church, the real Church, or any kind of exclusive elite. Whenever such tendencies appear, they are not the work of the Spirit that gave these movements birth.

## For God's Own Glory

The principle that God only acts for eternal purposes has other important consequences. It means, for example, that these movements of the Spirit are not primarily God's response to contemporary ills. They are not first to remedy the weaknesses of twentieth-century Christianity, nor to undo the blinkering effects of the Enlightenment with its closed-world system shut off from all sovereign divine activity. Nor are they primarily to overcome the negative effects of the Reformation and the Counter-Reformation. They do of course contribute to all these and more, but their scope cannot be reduced to them.

When God acts sovereignly, it is for the realization of the divine plan. Yes, of course, it will be a remedy for the ills of this age, and the way God acts in divine wisdom is shaped to reach the particular people to whom the Spirit comes. But God always acts for God and for Christ. 'The Father loves the Son, and has given all things into his hand' (John 3:35). The Father's love for the Son characterizes all the works of the Father. Anything less would be unworthy of God. 'For in him all things were created, in heaven and on earth, visible and invisible, whether thrones or dominions or principalities or authorities – all things were created through him *and for him*' (Col 1:16 italics mine). The Spirit is poured out to prepare the Church as the Bride of Christ, washed clean and sanctified for the wedding feast of the Lamb.

The Spirit is poured out for God's sake and for Christ's sake. It is a consequence of our self-centredness that we imagine God's purpose to be focused on ourselves. Isaiah 43 brings out the God-centredness of the work of creation and redemption: 'Every one who is called by my name, whom I created *for my glory*, whom I formed and made' (43:7); 'The people whom I formed *for myself* that they might declare my praise' (43:21); 'I, I am He who blots out your transgressions *for my own sake*, and I will not remember your sins' (43:25, all italics mine). God's redeeming work is to vindicate the holiness of his own name (see Ezek 20:44; 36:22–23, 32). That these are not evident truths reflects the degree to which we have lost a sense of the living God and the divine majesty.

This principle is all the more true of sovereign movements of God's grace that do not have human founders. They have in view the completion of all things and the recapitulation of all things under the headship of Christ. This perspective confirms what was said in Chapter Seven about the second coming of Christ. Every grace and gift of the Spirit of God is ordered of its nature towards the Parousia. Every corporate revival and movement is designed to prepare God's people for their final glorification as one body to the honour of Christ.

Several characteristics of these movements confirm

that the Lord is doing more than remedy the failings
of recent centuries. First, the ecumenical character of
this work of the Spirit has no precedent in Catholic–
Protestant history. It goes back in some sense behind all
post-Reformation controversies. Secondly, the restoration
of the spiritual gifts as part of the normal equipment of
every local church brings something not known in this
way since the first Christian centuries. This implies that
the Lord is here remedying something lost or drastically
weakened since the Constantinian era. Thirdly, the rise
of Messianic Judaism particularly illustrates this eschatological purpose, with the appearance for the first time
since the patristic period of a truly Jewish Christianity.
All these developments are manifestly of significance to
the entire body of Christ, which is itself for the sake of
all humanity.

# CHAPTER FOURTEEN

# THE PROMISES AND
# THE THREATS

Baptism in the Spirit brings a heightened awareness of the promises of God. The coming of the Holy Spirit in power awakens a living hope in God's promises. Indeed the Holy Spirit is described by Jesus as 'the promise of my Father' (Luke 24:49; see also Acts 1:4).

While the promises of God come quickly to life with the gift of the Spirit, the disasters threatened for the disobedient are less welcome and more easily ignored. However, the coming of the Spirit makes Christians more aware of the unholiness in the Church, and moves them to work for renewal and reform. Some have the painful experience of their personal renewal not being welcomed within their local church fellowship or of charismatic renewal being rejected or dismissed by unsympathetic pastors and church leaders. This lack of welcome can however be caused by immaturity and foolishness on the part of enthusiasts for renewal. Such tensions are among the factors causing some charismatic Christians to leave their Churches of upbringing to join Pentecostal or independent charismatic assemblies.

This division between 'traditional' Christians and those in new networks leads to opposed attitudes towards the mainline Churches: those who view them positively with loyalty and gratitude, and those who see them negatively with dismissal and even hostility. In this opposition, charismatic Christians within mainline Churches can fail to see their Churches as objects of God's judgment, while non-denominationals may simply see those same

Churches as objects of wrath, and no longer of mercy.
Such a separation is quite unscriptural.

It can be stated as a foundational principle that *the
promises and the threats are given by the Lord to the
same people*. This second principle is not just found in
the prophets, but throughout the Old Testament. To the
people of Israel, the message of the Lord is double-edged:
faith and obedience carry the divine promises and lead
to blessing; unbelief and disobedience carry God's curses
and lead to disaster and destruction. These are the terms
of the covenant, clearly set out in the summaries of
Leviticus 26 and Deuteronomy 28.

The initial understanding of Israel was that through
the covenant of Sinai, Yahweh became their God and they
became Yahweh's people. This clearly implied Yahweh's
blessing and protection, but required their obedience. The
Old Testament has several references to the breaking
of the covenant through Israel's rebellion: Exodus 32
has Moses shatter the tablets of the law following the
worship of the golden calf (Exod 32:19); the prophet
Hosea is instructed to name his son: 'Call his name
Not my people, for you are not my people and I am not
your God' (Hosea 1:9); the prophet Jeremiah pronounces
the Lord's rejection of the people who have broken the
covenant: 'I have forsaken my house, I have abandoned
my heritage; I have given the beloved of my soul into the
hands of her enemies. My heritage has become to me like
a lion in the forest, she has lifted up her voice against me;
therefore I hate her' (Jer 12:7–8).

A major departure from the secular model of political
treaties is the promise of reinstatement and restoration
following infraction of the covenant. It seems likely that
the original terms of the covenant did not mention this
possibility, and that God's call to return was revealed to
the people in their times of rebellion. There are several
renewals of the Sinai covenant described in the Old
Testament; some may be the addition of new generations
or new clusters of people entering the covenant, but some
are the reestablishment of what had been shattered
by sin. The remaking of the tablets of the law with

the renewal of the covenant (Exod 34:1, 10) follows the account of the rebellion in Exodus 32. This is also the context of the promise of the new covenant in Jeremiah 31. The renewals of the covenant reveal the amazing love of the Lord so graphically depicted in Isaiah 54:4–10: 'The Lord has called you like a wife forsaken and grieved in spirit, like a wife of youth when she is cast off, says your God' (54:6).

In Deuteronomy the possibility of restoration is mentioned separately (ch. 30) from the lists of blessings and curses (ch. 28), which may reflect a later addition. The book of Leviticus, later in its final redaction than Deuteronomy, integrates the possibility of restoration into the covenant blessings and curses:

If then their uncircumcised heart is humbled and they make amends for their iniquity; then I will remember my covenant with Jacob, and I will remember my covenant with Isaac and my covenant with Abraham, and I will remember the land. But the land shall be left by them, and enjoy its sabbaths while it lies desolate without them; and they shall make amends for their iniquity, because they spurned my ordinances, and their soul abhorred my statutes. Yet for all that, when they are in the land of their enemies, I will not spurn them, neither will I abhor them so as to destroy them utterly and break my covenant with them; for I am the Lord their God; but I will for their sake remember the covenant with their forefathers, whom I brought forth out of the land of Egypt in the sight of the nations, that I might be their God: I am the Lord. (Lev 26:41–45)

As the people of Israel and Judah kept on hearing the call to repentance and restoration after their repeated periods of rebellion, they were led to reflect more deeply on God's unfailing love (*hesed*) and faithfulness (*emet*). 'Return to the Lord, your God, for he is gracious and merciful, slow to anger, and abounding in steadfast love, and repents of evil' (Joel 2:13). More attention came to

be paid to the unconditional promises to Abraham and
to David. Thus the covenant with David that will not be
withdrawn (2 Sam 7:15–16) is recalled by the prophets
(Jer 33:14–17; Ezek 34:23; Zech 6:12). There are signs of
a growing awareness of the importance of the covenant
with Abraham (Ps 105:9, 42; Isa 41:8; 51:2; Dan 3:35).
It is this theme that reappears with great force in the
canticles in Luke's infancy gospel (Luke 1:55, 72–73).
Here we can see the germs of Paul's teaching in Galatians
that justification is by faith in the promise rather than by
good works based on observance of the law.

## Prophetic Denunciations and Promises

In the prophetic writings, denunciations of faithless Israel
and Judah are regularly followed by the promise of restoration. The strong message of Amos against the sins
of Israel ends with the prophecy of restoration (Amos
9:13–15). The indictment of Jeremiah 2:1–3:13 is followed
by the promises of 3:14–18; the complaints of 3:19–5:17 by
the promise: 'But even in those days, says the Lord, I will
not make a full end of you' (5:18). The denunciations of
chs 7–12:13 are followed by a characteristic passage:

> Thus says the Lord concerning all my evil neighbours
> who touch the heritage which I have given my people
> Israel to inherit: 'Behold, I will pluck them up from
> their land, and I will pluck up the house of Judah
> from among them. And after I have plucked them
> up, I will again have compassion on them, and I will
> bring them again each to his heritage and each to his
> land. (Jer 12:14–15)

A similar pattern can be found in the later chapters of
Hosea. After several chapters of denunciation and threats
(4–10), we find an astonishing revelation of the heart of
Yahweh for his rebellious people:

> How can I give you up, O Ephraim!
> How can I hand you over, O Israel!

How can I make you like Admah!
How can I treat you like Zeboiim!
My heart recoils within me,
my compassion grows warm and tender.
I will not execute my fierce anger,
I will not again destroy Ephraim;
for I am God and not man,
the Holy One in your midst,
and I will not come to destroy.
They shall go after the Lord,
he will roar like a lion;
yea, he will roar,
and his sons shall come trembling from the west;
they shall come trembling like birds from Egypt,
and like doves from the land of Assyria;
and I will return them to their homes, says the Lord.
(Hosea 11:8–11)

The woes against Judah and Jerusalem pronounced by
Zephaniah are followed by the promise of Messianic blessings (Zeph 3:11–20). Finally in the last of the prophetic
books, the rebukes of the Lord (Mal 2:1–9) are followed
by the promise of judgment leading to destruction or
cleansing and healing (Mal 3:2–4; 3:17–4:2).

## Restoration of the One Inheritance

The promise is to those who have suffered the calamity.
God will rebuild these ruins, the ruins of his ancient
city. The people will be brought back to this land, the
land promised and given to their forefathers. The depth
of corruption and the extent of the devastation does
not deter the Lord, who is set on vindicating his Holy
Name.

It is unbiblical to adopt any dichotomy that says in
effect: you people sinned and have lost the inheritance;
we haven't and are now the heirs. This is a weakness of
some restorationist positions, which pick out the rejection
of Saul and his replacement by David without grasping
the fundamental relationship between covenant promises

and threats. But equally wrong is the complacency of the mainline Churches, which does not see and grieve over their own sin, and which treats the inheritance as a possession they cannot lose. In the same way, the charismatic renewal in the mainline Churches is weak wherever it fails to be prophetic, and does not humbly address and lament the sins of the people, both in the charismatic renewal and in one's own Church.

God remains wholly faithful to whatever witness there is of the Holy Spirit in each Christian family and tradition. That witness is the bearer of the divine promise. It is the responsibility of each Church to purify its own faith, so that the true work of the Spirit of God in its tradition may shine forth. Work for Christian unity and the quest for profound renewal are ultimately inseparable. This was clearly grasped in the Vatican Council Decree on Ecumenism in its section on 'spiritual ecumenism'. 'Every renewal of the Church essentially consists in an increase of fidelity to her own calling' (para 6).

The quest for fidelity to the work of the Spirit in one's own Church tradition cannot be pursued in isolation, for this task sends all Churches back to the one Jesus, the one Spirit, the one Word of God. All are heirs both of the promises and of the threats, which both precede the divisions. As we heed the threats together, so we prepare to receive the promises together.

## CHAPTER FIFTEEN

# THE REMNANT AND THE SUFFERING SERVANT

Throughout the rebellious history of Israel and Judah, there were always those who remained faithful to the covenant, though often few in number. So the Lord promised Elijah: 'Yet I will leave seven thousand in Israel, all the knees that have not bowed to Baal, and every mouth that has not kissed him.' (1 Kings 19:18). The true prophets exemplify faithful resistance to idolatry and infidelity. They witness to the demands of the covenant and they warn of impending disaster should the people not repent for their evil ways.

In the first five centuries of the monarchy, the voice of the prophets became stronger as the people of Israel and Judah lapsed further into rebellion and sin. This very fact – greater sin and more prophecy – was itself a measure of the depth of God's love for his covenant people. The great prophets (Jeremiah, Deutero-Isaiah and Ezekiel) spoke the Word of the Lord in the midst of the evils brought on by the people's disobedience.

The faithful few who did not bend the knee to Baal always identified themselves fully with the chosen people and their call. They did not perceive themselves as an élite, or as replacements for unfaithful kings and priests. Even when the prophetic word from the Lord pronounced a judgment of rejection upon Israel and Judah, this never excluded the possibility of repentance or revoked the divine promise to this people. Through all the human stubborness and God's unfailing patience, God was working his purpose out and preparing the way for the full realization of his Kingdom. Though this is not a linear progress, the intensification of God's self-investment involved new stages, involving surprising new developments, but they always built on the promises already given. Thus the prophets, the wisdom teaching and the apocalyptic visions of the Old Testament represent new stages in the outworking of the promise given to Abraham, of the covenant made with Moses, of the promise of the kingdom given to David.

## The Role of the Faithful Remnant

The faithful few, often represented by the prophets, are the authentic bearers of the promise. They provide the continuity not just of flesh and blood, but of spirit. The revelation to Israel grows and develops in this continuous current of heroic faith among the few. It was in these circles that the books of the Old Testament took shape.

The concept of the *faithful remnant* developed among this minority who remained true to the covenant with Yahweh. Initially the remnant may refer simply to those Jews who survived the tragedies of war, devastation and exile. 'And he who is left in Zion and remains in Jerusalem will be called holy, every one who has been recorded for life in Jerusalem' (Isa 4:3). But those who survive carry the promise. So there is a link between the remnant that survives the exile and the remnant that is faithful to the covenant. 'I will surely gather all of you, O Jacob, I will gather the remnant of Israel' (Micah 2:12).

The identification of God's faithful servants with the inheritance and the destiny of the chosen people is shown in their times of loss and suffering. When Israel, Judah and Jerusalem suffer devastation because of their disobedience to the Lord, the faithful suffer with them. Jeremiah even accompanies the people to Egypt after prophesying death if they went to Egypt in distrust of the Lord's promises (Jer 43:7–8). Ezekiel joins the exiles in Babylon. This solidarity is expressed above all in the tragic beauty of the book of Lamentations: 'How lonely sits the city that was full of people! How like a widow has she become, she that was great among the nations! She that was a princess among the cities has become a vassal' (Lam 1:1). The lamentations are so poignant because they capture the intense grief of the faithful Israelite who loves the Lord's people and the holy city but who recognizes the terrible tragedy of the people's infidelity.

In the Lamentations of Jeremiah, the faithful grieve over Israel's and Judah's disobedience; they acknowledge the justice in this punishment: 'The Lord has done what he purposed, has carried out his threat; as he ordained long ago, he has demolished without pity; he has made the enemy rejoice over you, and exalted the might of your foes' (Lam 2:17). But through this lament there runs a faith in the living God, that cannot deny the goodness of the Lord, and that recognizes the Lord's compassion: 'For the Lord will not cast off for ever, but, though he cause grief, he will have compassion according to the abundance of his steadfast love; for he does not willingly afflict or grieve the sons of men' (Lam 3:31–33).

## The Suffering Servant

Thus the leaders who wail for the sins of the whole people (Jeremiah, Nehemiah, Baruch, Daniel) not only keep the covenant and inherit the promise; they suffer at the hands of the sinful majority. There is in this faithful remnant a double form of suffering: first, enduring the punishment of God for the sins of all ('the Lord has made her suffer for the multitude of her transgressions' Lam 1:5); and second, they are persecuted by the majority for their fidelity to the covenant. So Jeremiah suffers constant harassment, is thrown into a muddy cistern, and placed in the stocks.

In this context appears the astonishing figure of the suffering servant. The four servant songs in Isaiah are not simply messianic prophecies but also express a profound sense of what the Lord was doing among his people at the time of their composition. They express the faith experience of the faithful remnant. So one song identifies the servant with Israel: 'And he said to me, "You are my servant, Israel, in whom I will be glorified" (Isa 49:3).

In the servant songs, the promise of future restoration is linked with the suffering of the faithful servant. The one, whom God formed 'from the womb to be his servant, to bring Jacob back to him, and that Israel might be gathered to him' (Isa 49:5) is the one who will say: 'I gave my back to the smiters, and my cheeks to those who pulled out the beard; I hid not my face from shame and spitting' (Isa 50:6). This connection is even more explicit in the fourth song (Isa 52:13–53:12).

There is here a profound mystery of election and rejection. The faithful remnant manifest the election of the elect. But it is the faithful servants who are rejected and persecuted. In this, the faithful remnant foreshadows Jesus, who is both the Chosen One of God, in whom the Father is well pleased, and the Rejected One, who cries out from the cross: 'My God, my God, why hast thou forsaken me?' (Ps 22:1).

Jesus is the one who totally identifies with sinful humanity, and undergoes a baptism of repentance for all. Jesus is the suffering servant who embodies the hope of Israel and who suffers for his total fidelity to God. He is the Holy One of Israel who makes his own the great prayers of repentance for the sins of all, because he has taken their nature and identified himself with them in their alienation from God. All that is said about God punishing his people is visited upon Jesus. What is said in Lamentations about the destruction of Zion can be applied (apart from the breaking of bones) to the destruction of the man Jesus:

I am the man who has seen affliction
under the rod of his wrath;
he has driven and brought me
into darkness without any light;
surely against me he turns his hand
again and again the whole day long.
He has made my flesh and my skin waste away,
and broken my bones;
he has besieged and enveloped me
with bitterness and tribulation;

> he has made me dwell in darkness
> like the dead of long ago. (Lam 3:1–6)

All the disasters threatened for disobedience to the covenant are taken upon his shoulders by Jesus. In his death on the cross, Jesus experiences the effects of sin in all their stark horror. He is at the same time the one faithful keeper of the covenant, and the one who tastes the full effects of Sin. In God's perfect wisdom, the punishment and rejection then become the very instrument by which God effects the salvation and deliverance of all.

In the paradoxical combination of election and rejection, there is both manifestation and hiddenness. From the outward theophany of Sinai and the glorious consecration of the Temple in Jerusalem, there is a process of concentration that leads to the faithful remnant and the suffering servant. This process reaches its climax in God's sovereign intervention in the Incarnation, which takes place in humble obscurity. The revelation-manifestation and the emptying (*kenosis*) are inextricable, a paradox which is most fully expressed in the glory of the cross. The removal of all veils, and the full manifestation of the Lord without any hiddenness belongs to the second coming (Col 3:4).

## Resumé of Old Testament Principles

We can now summarize the general principles concerning God's dealings with his people in their mixed history of obedience and rebellion, of heroes of faith and villains of disobedience and idolatry:

(1)  God chooses Israel as a priestly people in order to save and bless all nations;

(2)  God punishes all rebellion and disobedience;

(3)  the rebellion of the chosen people does not deflect God's purpose, nor does it weaken the divine love for those God has marked with his name;

(4)  the divine favour and the divine promises are wholly undeserved;

(5)   God's faithfulness is founded in God not in Israel; God's work of deliverance is for God's glory and the vindication of his holy Name;

(6)   the chosen people are at one and the same time sinners called to repentance and children of the promises;

(7)   the fidelity of the remnant under persecution becomes the instrument whereby the inheritance is passed on and the promise is fulfilled; this is God's preparation for the salvation of all peoples through Jesus, the suffering servant who embodies the fidelity of Israel;

(8)   the process of developing revelation involves a combination of sovereign intervention and of hiddenness, which will characterize the period of the Church.

# CHAPTER SIXTEEN

# REMEMBER ABRAHAM, YOUR FATHER

The issues of the new and the old, the continuous and the discontinuous, the promises and the threats, election and rejection, raise the question of tradition. Seeing the inter-connection between all these elements will protect Christians from many dangers; of rigid attachment to the old and of uncritical enthusiasm for the new; of complacency as the chosen and of disdain towards other Christians.

For the Pentecostal and charismatic movements, the question ought not to be 'old or new?' but how to discern what is of the Spirit both in the new and in the old. Antiquity and novelty are of themselves indications neither of the presence nor of the absence of the Holy Spirit. Authentic revival and renewal involve a fresh interaction between the new and the old. Obedience to the covenant is never simply adherence to a fixed code, but fidelity to a developing relationship with the living God.

In the search for biblical guidelines for discernment, the writings of the Old Testament prophets are of special relevance. They depict a situation of drastic decline and corruption, together with a radical new work of God in the prophets recalling God's abiding promises to the people chosen of old. All the essential ingredients are present: serious decline, new intervention of God, long-standing inheritance.

## A Word to the Dispossessed

'Hearken to me, you who pursue deliverance,
   you who seek the Lord;

look to the rock from which you were hewn,
     and to the quarry from which you were digged.
Look to Abraham your father
     and to Sarah who bore you;
for when he was but one I called him,
     and I blessed him and made him many.
For the Lord will comfort Zion;
     he will comfort all her waste places,
and will make her wilderness like Eden,
     her desert like the garden of the Lord;
joy and gladness will be found in her,
     thanksgiving and the voice of song.' (Isa 51:1–3)

This word of the Lord could serve as a charter for Church
renewal. It was addressed to God's people at a time of
intense suffering. Previous chapters in Isaiah had spoken
of 'your waste and your desolate places and your devastated
land' (49:19) and of the people's punishment: 'Where is your
mother's bill of divorce, with which I put her away? Or
which of my creditors is it to whom I have sold you? Behold,
for your iniquities you were sold, and for your transgressions your mother was put away' (50:1). In this situation,
the prophet has a word for all concerned with renewal of
the people's life and the restoration of their inheritance.

The first command is to 'look to the rock from which
you were hewn, and to the quarry from which you were
digged' (51:1). None of us are simply regenerated from
heaven, without earthly forebears. We are all hewn from
an existing rock. The next sentence makes this more
explicit: 'Look to Abraham your father and to Sarah
who bore you' (51:2).

That is to say, we have fathers and mothers in the
faith. We are born into a people, into a family descended
from one father – Abraham in the Old Covenant, God the
Father through Jesus in the New. Renewal always goes
back to the origins, and reaffirms them. This applies at
every level in the Christian life:

• for the renewal of the whole Church, going back to the
  biblical origins;

- for particular Church traditions, going back to the work of God in their founder-figures;
- for a religious order, a movement or a community, going back to the charisms of the origins;
- for each Christian, going back to God's foundational acts in baptism–regeneration–conversion, in baptism in the Spirit, and in calls to specific forms of service or ways of life.

The first reason for going back to the origins is the faithfulness of God. When the Lord begins a new work, whether corporate or personal, the Spirit always acts in view of God's final purpose. The foundations laid by the Lord are the only possible foundations for what remains God's work. The way back from disobedience is always to return to the Lord's foundations.

This is why memorial (*anamnesis*) is so central to Christian life and practice. Our faithfulness always involves recalling to mind the acts of God on our behalf since the beginning. In the early chapters of Deuteronomy, the Israelites are constantly urged to remember and not to forget, and in the prophets, Israel's sin is described in terms of forgetting God (Jer 3:21). This command to remember is a kind of extension of the fourth commandment: 'Honour your father and your mother, that your days may be long in the land which the Lord your God gives you' (Exod 20:12; see also Deut 5:16).

## Knowing Our Fathers and Mothers in the Faith

True renewal involves identifying and knowing our fathers and mothers in the faith. Each Christian needs to know his/her own personal history of faith. Each community must know its roots and draw from them. Each community of faith at whatever level needs to ask: Who are our fathers and mothers in the faith? Who are those precursors whose life and teaching have shaped the Christianity that we have imbibed?

This question applies to all Christians, not just to those

who formally venerate tradition. For some groupings, the fathers and mothers in the faith may be leaders of movements and currents of revival rather than Church leaders. Even those who say they simply believe in the Bible have been shaped and formed by those who evangelized and taught them, and by those whose translations and annotations of the Bible they use.

We are all reborn into a family of faith. The particular Christianity we represent is like a family inheritance. It has features common to every family and features peculiar to itself. We do not just believe in a list of doctrines, but we receive a body of convictions that anchor a way of life. The doctrines our family believes have a context, and different family contexts have their distinct emphases. These are rarely our own creation, even in many new non-denominational groups. They come down to us from our fathers and mothers in the faith.

Remembering and revering our fathers and mothers in the faith is neither mere imitation nor mimicry. It is to know how God dealt with them, and blessed them. It is identifying their gifts, their charisms, their anointings. It is identifying all the ways in which God shaped our tradition, our spiritual family. It means knowing this past work of the Lord so as to allow the Holy Spirit to impress the same realities upon us, their spiritual children. The result is not cloning, but the creative handing on of a living faith tradition in love and fidelity.

The Lord who summoned the Jews to remember Abraham their father and Sarah their mother was doing a new thing in their midst. The Babylonian exile lies at the origin of that distinctively Jewish institution, the synagogue, that was to play an important role in the life of Jesus and in the formation of the Christian Church. This shows that the Christian life is never totally reducible to memory and tradition; it is as we receive the inheritance in faith that we experience the new blessings of the Lord.

## The Church Our Mother

The mention of Sarah the mother has its own significance. For as Abraham is a type of the heavenly Father (as in the offering of Isaac) so Sarah is a type of the Church, as Paul teaches in Galatians 4. Christian re-birth is not simply the act of the Father without any mother. Rather God engenders new life, regenerates new sons and daughters for eternal life, through a mother: through the Church that God has brought into being. However, it is significant that Paul speaks not of the earthly Church as our mother, 'but the Jerusalem above is free, and she is our mother' (Gal 4:26). In Galatians, the covenant transference is not from Israel to the Church militant on earth, but from the old earthly inheritance to the new and heavenly kingdom, the same transposition that characterizes the letter to the Hebrews.

This emphasis on the heavenly Jerusalem as our mother does not invalidate the application of Isaiah 51 to the Christian Church. But it is a sharp reminder that the Church on earth is not a self-contained entity, but the earthly manifestation of an essentially heavenly reality shaped by the Holy Spirit. It is this divine-human heavenly-earthly Church that is the mother of each Christian. To this Church and to the local embodiment in which the new life was born, the words of Psalm 87 about Zion can be applied: '"This one and that one were born in her"; for the Most High himself will establish her' (87:5).

Because our mother is the heavenly Jerusalem, what we have to recall and revere is precisely that which on earth belongs to heaven: that is to say, the work of the Holy Spirit in the Church, in the denomination, in the religious order, in the revival-renewal movement, in the individual. It is the work of the Holy Spirit in our origins that is to be identified, cherished and built upon.

For each Christian, the understanding and practice of the faith is strongly marked by the traditions in which we have been formed. The patterns of worship we have experienced, the hymns we have sung, the types of preaching and teaching we have heard, the ways the Bible has been used, the ways in which authority has been exercised, the moral emphases we have internalized; all these and more are mediated through the various Christian traditions. This coloration is always greater than we realize, even extending to the ways we rebel against our own upbringing.

## The Comforting of Zion

The command to remember and revere Abraham and Sarah is followed by a promise for the holy city. 'For the Lord will comfort Zion; he will comfort all her waste places, and will make her wilderness like Eden, her desert like the garden of the Lord; joy and gladness will be found in her, thanksgiving and the voice of song' (Isa 51:3). This evocation of Eden, the garden of the Lord, illustrates the fundamental principle that God's purpose is not deflected by sin. In the work of redemption, God the Creator effects the reintegration of the wayward sinner into the divine purpose established 'before the foundation of the world' (Eph 1:4). The wilderness caused by sin is to be remade like the paradise of God. The devastation wrought by infidelity among God's people will be transformed into the paradise of God, into the Son in whom the Father is well pleased, as the people turn back to Abraham their father and Sarah their mother.

There is a striking contrast between the present desolation and the future abundance. The prophecy is given at a time of the deepest gloom and the most intense suffering. The holy city is desolate. It is in the midst of this devastation that the Lord promises a glorious restoration.

Compare this contrast to the present situation in the Churches. Most Christians in the mainline Churches praying for renewal do not see their Churches as a devastated city or a spiritual wilderness. They probably think of dullness needing enlivening, or weakness needing remedial treatment. By contrast, those who see the older Churches as wastelands have probably left them for new pastures, dismissing denominational or Church renewal as a mirage for naive optimists. The Christian who truly knows both the glory of the Lord and the heart of man will be like the great prophets of the Old Testament who both saw the devastation of Jerusalem and proclaimed her future restoration.

# CHAPTER SEVENTEEN

# REPENTING FOR THE SINS OF THE PEOPLE

In the Old Testament, the leaders and prophets faithful to the Lord grieve deeply for the pitiful condition of God's chosen people. Their love for the Lord and the covenant leads to deep lamentation for the sins that have laid the people low. The identification of God's servants with the whole people includes identification with their sins.

When Nehemiah received news in Babylon of the sad condition of Judah and Jerusalem, he sat down and wept, and mourned for days (Neh 1:2–4). His response was characteristic of the faithful Jewish leader:

> Let your ear be attentive, and your eyes open, to hear the prayer of your servant which I now pray before you day and night for the people of Israel your servants, confessing the sins of the people of Israel, which we have sinned against you. Yea, I and my father's house have sinned. We have acted very corruptly against you, and have not kept the commandments, the statutes, and the ordinances which you commanded your servant Moses. (Neh 1:6–7)

In a situation of grave apostasy, the faithful Daniel prays in a similar way to Nehemiah: 'All Israel has transgressed your law and turned aside, refusing to obey your voice. And the curse and oath which are written in the law of Moses the servant of God have been poured out upon us, because we have sinned against him' (Dan 9:11).

In these prayers of repentance, the faithful servants (Nehemiah, Daniel) confess that the plight of Israel is the result of the people's sin, which is the sin of all, including themselves. The justice of God's punishment is acknowledged. Their prayers express a vivid sense of the offence against God involved in this rebellion.

Like all zealous reformers, Nehemiah and the author of Daniel were disgusted with the corruption they saw around them. But they were humble enough to see that they were not exempt from the tendencies they deplored. They make no attempt to exonerate themselves from this judgment. So Nehemiah confesses: 'I and my father's house have sinned' (Neh 1:6); himself first, and everyone else in second place. This marks out the truly spiritual leader from the merely angry reformer or dissident.

Holy people have always known that the closer they come to the all-holy God, the more they know they are guilty of the very things in the Church that make them ashamed. Non-observance of the laws of worship is reflected every time we do not turn to prayer. Persecution of the prophets is a more violent expression of every refusal to hear the word of God. Greed and bribery among the people are echoed whenever financial concerns are placed before the Lord's purpose. Violence unleashed against fellow believers is repeated in our own acts of prejudice. Every mentality of ecclesiastical self-sufficiency ('I have no need of you' 1 Cor 12:21) finds its counterpart in our failure to recognize the Lord in other Christians and in our 'go-it-alone' behaviour that ignores their existence.

## Repenting for the Sins of the Fathers

This prophetic identification with the sins of the people is not restricted to the present generation. For the Old Testament prophets, an essential element of restoration is *repentance* for the sins of their fathers. The covenant people experience a solidarity both in obedience to God and in repentance for sin. The rebellion of one generation is not independent of the rebellion of their ancestors. Ezekiel 20 shows how Judah's sin followed in the footsteps of their fathers in the wilderness. The prophet demands: 'Wherefore say to the house of Israel, Thus says the Lord God: Will you defile yourselves after the manner of your fathers and go astray after their detestable things?' (Ezek 20:30).

The prophets and people convicted of their sin recognized this solidarity with their fathers. 'We have sinned against the Lord our God, we and our fathers, from our youth even to this day; and we have not obeyed the voice of the Lord our God' (Jer 3:25). 'To us, O Lord, belongs confusion of face, to our kings, to our princes, and to our fathers, because we have sinned against you' (Dan 9:8).

What does it mean to repent for the sins of our fathers? In the context of divided Christianity, it includes repentance for all the ways we have inherited from our fathers that cause scandal and division. We have certainly inherited the treasure of God's Word and the riches of Christian worship and devotion; a rich diversity of liturgy and sacraments, of gifts and ministries, of patterns of service to the Lord and to the needy. But we have also inherited the weaknesses and blind spots of our fathers. We have taken on their prejudices and hostilities towards other Christians, their false oppositions and distorted emphases, their over-simplifications. We have not only received them; we have often welcomed them with enthusiasm.

It is easiest to see that we must repent for the areas of our weakness. For example, Catholics are led to repent for neglect of God's Word in the past, in theology and in devotions; and for exercises of spiritual authority in ways alien to the Spirit of Jesus. Protestants may be led to repent for their suspicion of authority, a neglect of the body of Christ, and a suspicion of all outward forms. But we should also be open to repentance in the areas that we regard as our strengths. For often the ways we have practised and taught the strong areas (e.g. Catholic teaching on the eucharist, Protestant teaching on justification by faith) have made it more difficult for other

Christians to receive the Spirit's gift in that teaching. Often the accentuation of distinctive doctrines has caused distortion within the whole framework of Christian faith. Thus a Catholic focus on Catholic distinctives such as eucharistic sacrifice, Mary and papal primacy easily leads to distortion of these doctrines. Protestant concentration on the sole authority of the Scriptures can end up by damaging the very Word that it seeks to defend.

Our repentance for the sins of our fathers involves this recognition that what they did and thought, we have done and thought. We abandon all pretence to being a privileged generation, somehow more enlightened, less given to the frailties and abominations of our ancestors. Some of the greatest horrors of all time have been perpetrated in the twentieth century. When respected Church leaders truly repent from the heart, it has a power to touch people, like the prayer of Nehemiah, who was doubtless seen by the people as a pillar of righteousness.

How does this apply to the life of the Churches? The history of each Church typically manifests repeated patterns of rebellion, inflexibility, self-sufficiency, self-righteousness, similar to that of the Israelites in the desert and in the Promised Land. Like Israel, each Church is tempted to 'trust in [its own] beauty' (Ezek 16:15). Even the most hallowed of our traditions can become the object of this self-love. So Catholics and Orthodox can pride themselves on the wealth of church tradition, on the majesty of *our* liturgy, on the depth of *our* theology, while Protestants can acclaim themselves for the purity of *our* gospel and *our* devotion to the Scriptures. Whenever we love the greatness of our tradition, not seeing the real richness as total gift constantly threatened by our sin, we are loving our own beauty instead of the Lord. We are offering ourselves for admiration, rather than the Lord for worship.

It is a sad fact that corporate repentance for the sins of our Churches appears to be a rare event. In 1965, Pope Paul VI and Patriarch Athenagoras both regretted 'the offensive words, the reproaches without foundation and the reprehensible gestures . . . on both sides' at

the time of the split between East and West in 1054.[1]
But this posture has not deeply entered the life of the
Churches. It has not extended to the sphere of ordinary
Church practice, of theology and worship. Nor sadly has
it yet become a regular element in theological dialogue
between the Churches. All the Churches are called to
be both humble and responsible – before God. Bringing
Church life to the judgment seat of God will pierce the
veils of defensiveness and self-sufficiency.

When we repent for our sin, God restores our inheritance. As each Church lives from the Spirit's gift, it will
be more disposed to accept the work of the same Spirit
in other Churches. The grace of repentance is part of the
grace of reconciliation. As the Churches repent for their
sins against the Lord and against each other, there will
be reconciliation, by various stages as the repentance
deepens and takes root in the embodied life of each
Church. Then all will be led into the fulness of that
inheritance, which sin and division have fragmented and
defiled.

# CHAPTER EIGHTEEN

# THE PIVOTAL ROLE OF ISRAEL

The paradox of election and rejection, first addressed in Chapter Fifteen on the faithful remnant and the suffering servant, becomes most acute in the refusal of Israel as a whole to accept Jesus as the Messiah.

This inextricable mixture of fidelity and infidelity, of divine promises and divine punishment, of election and rejection, especially occupied the mind of the apostle Paul. Paul, the converted Pharisee, steeped in all the traditions of the Law, grappled with one question above all: 'I ask, then, has God rejected his people?' (Rom 11:1). After many centuries of exclusively Gentile Christianity, we do not easily grasp the agony and the force in this question. It brings home how different the fulfilment of the Messianic promise was to all Jewish expectation. Not only did the coming of the Messiah bring full admission to the Gentiles, but it was only accepted by a minority among the Jews.

Paul's question is similar to that posed by Christians who are tempted to despair of historic Christianity, whether in its Catholic, Orthodox, Anglican or Protestant forms. Has God rejected the Churches of East and West that trace their origins back to the apostolic age? Has God rejected the work of the Spirit in the Protestant Reformation? Paul's answer to his question about Israel should, I am convinced, also be ours. 'By no means! I myself am an Israelite, a descendant of Abraham, a member of the tribe of Benjamin' (Rom 11:1).

Not only is Paul's answer relevant to present-day issues of election and rejection, but his argumentation is still applicable, *mutatis mutandis*. Paul is insistent that God never goes back on his Word, but is ever faithful to his promises. 'But it is not as though the word of God had failed. For not all who are descended from Israel belong to Israel' (Rom 9:6). Paul invokes the concept of the faithful remnant (9:27; 11:2–5) to argue that this minority is the vehicle of the divine promises, because the real Israel are the ones who live by grace through faith (these chapters come in the letter to the Romans dealing with justification by faith). In the midst of the physical Israel is the spiritual Israel that in faith continues to receive the promise.

What then of the unfaithful majority? Are they rejected? Paul faces this question directly in Chapter 11: 'What then? Israel failed to obtain what it sought. The elect obtained it, but the rest were hardened' (11:7). 'So I ask, have they stumbled so as to fall?' (11:11). In other words, are the Jews who did not accept Jesus as Messiah rejected by God? Again Paul gives the same emphatic response: 'By no means!'. He then advances a remarkable argument: 'But through their trespass salvation has come to the Gentiles, so as to make Israel jealous. Now if their trespass means riches for the world, and if their failure means riches for the Gentiles, how much more will their full inclusion mean!' (11:11–12).[1]

In the astonishing providence of God, the very hard-heartedness of the chosen people becomes the means by which God saves all, first the Gentiles and then the Jews. So if the rejection by the Jews produces 'riches for the world' then how much more wonderful will be the blessings accompanying their eventual reintegration. This teaching is reinforced by the imagery of olive trees, natural and wild: the Gentile believers are like wild olive branches grafted on the natural olive after many of the natural branches have been cut off. In this analogy, the severed branches retain a natural aptitude to be grafted back on to the tree; that is to say, the Israel that has not accepted Jesus as the Messiah has an ongoing inner orientation to reintegration. In fact Paul goes beyond aptitude to state: 'And even the others, if they do not persist in their unbelief, will be grafted in, for God has the power to graft them in again' (Rom 11:23). At this point Paul makes a similar statement to verse 12, emphasizing that the reintegration of Israel is a lesser thing for God than the ingrafting of the Gentiles: 'For if you have been cut from what is by nature a wild olive tree, and grafted, contrary to nature, into a cultivated olive tree, how much more will these natural branches be grafted back into their own olive tree' (Rom 11:24).

Paul now goes beyond the conditional affirmation of Israel's salvation (v 23) to an unqualified prophecy concerning the final salvation of Israel: 'Lest you be wise in your own conceits, I want you to understand this mystery, brethren: a hardening has come upon part of Israel, until the full number of the Gentiles come in, and so all Israel will be saved' (Rom 11:25–26). There is, Paul is saying, a direct link between Christ's rejection by the majority of his people and the salvation of the Gentiles, so he writes: 'Just as you were once disobedient to God but now have received mercy because of their disobedience, so they have now been disobedient in order that by the mercy shown to you they also may receive mercy' (Rom 11:30–31).

Paul is almost revelling in paradox. The writing off of the Jews by Gentile Christians echoes Jewish dismissal of the Gentiles. Both forms of logical narrowness are denied by the extraordinary mercy and wisdom of God. None can boast. All are disobedient. All are graced through sheer mercy. 'For God has consigned all men to disobedience, that he may have mercy upon all' (Rom 11:32).

For Paul, then, the promises of God to Israel endure. The original promise of restoration following repentance still stands (Rom 11:23). Even though the Jews who rejected Jesus are 'enemies of God' as regards the gospel, 'as regards election they are beloved for the sake of their forefathers' (Rom 11:28). They remain 'chosen'; they remain Israelites, to whom 'belong the sonship, the glory, the covenants, the giving of the law, the worship, and the promises; to them belong the patriarchs, and of their race, according to the flesh, is the Christ. God who is over all be blessed for ever. Amen' (Rom 9:4–5). Israel's place in God's plan is not cancelled. All this is

most sure for one reason: 'the gifts and the call of God
are irrevocable' (Rom 11:29).

## Implications for the Churches

What bearing does Paul's teaching on Israel have on the
problems of corruption and deviation in the Churches,
on Christian division, on Church renewal and on the
proliferation of new denominations and groupings? As
we have already seen, Paul's teaching builds on that
of the Old Testament, of Israel being a priestly people
called for the sake of all nations, of the faithful remnant
who embody the heart of the tradition and who are its
authentic witnesses.

Perhaps we can focus this question by asking: What
parallels are there between Christ's coming in relation to
Israel and the Gentiles on the one hand, and the outpouring of the Holy Spirit in pentecostal blessing in relation
to the mainline Churches and new non-denominational
groupings on the other hand?

First of all, let us note the clear differences. First, there
is only one Incarnation. Jesus' death, resurrection and
ascension are unique. The comings of the Holy Spirit give
believers a share in the unique event and life of Jesus
Christ, first through the unique foundational event of
Pentecost. No subsequent outpouring of the Spirit prior
to the Parousia captures everything contained in the one
full event of the Incarnation of the Son of God.

Secondly, Israel is the bearer of the promise, whereas
the Church is the fruit and witness to initial fulfilment
and to remaining promise. Thus there is not a total
equivalence between Israel before Christ and the Church
after Christ. So, for example, while Israel has always
had a more precise identity than the Gentiles or nations,
the statements in Romans 9–11 about the Gentiles are
generic, not about specific groups or traditions.

Nonetheless, there are important principles expressed
in Romans 11 which have a direct bearing on the new
patterns of unity and division occurring in the Pentecostal
and charismatic movements. It is these principles that

have enduring relevance that we seek to distil from Paul's treatment of God's fidelity to Israel. We have already seen from the Old Testament that the chosen are called on behalf of all and that the faithful believer in the midst of a sinful people identifies fully with its calling and true heritage. Romans 11 adds the following:

(1) There is a clear enunciation of the principle that God's gifts and call are irrevocable. This principle rules out all those theologies of replacement, whereby new groupings of Christians unchurch the ancient Churches and pronounce them excluded from God's inheritance. This does not mean that God may not call some Christians to separate, just as the separation of the Northern Kingdom of Israel was authenticated by the prophetic word of Ahijah (1 Kings 11:31–39). But it does mean that the body from which they come out remains within the purpose of God, whose promises are not voided by sin and corruption.

(2) A rather less clear but undoubted link is made between the destiny of the graced and that of the disgraced. The whole thrust of Romans 11 is that no one grouping can boast of being graced by God, for all have been disobedient, and their gracing is the sheer mercy of an ever-loving God. Moreover, in God's inscrutable wisdom, the very disobedience of one bloc can become the occasion of grace for another.

Is there a suggestion here that the final salvation of Israel may be linked in some way with the disobedience and apostasy of the nations? This is not explicitly stated. However, the principle formulated in Romans 11:32 could have such an application. It would then be confirmed by the New Testament passages which speak of a falling away in the last days; these include Luke 12:45; 18:8; 2 Thess 2:3–4; 1 Tim 4:1; 2 Tim 3:1; 2 Peter 3:3, Jude 18. This partly depends on the meaning of the phrase 'until the full number of the Gentiles [*tó pléróma tón ethnón*] come in' (Rom 11:25). The preferable interpretation, according better with the meaning of *pléróma* elsewhere in Paul, would take *pléróma* in the sense of the fulness of God's plan involving all the nations, rather than envisaging the whole world becoming Christian.

This view of divine providence opens the door to Christians of all persuasions to recognize the Holy Spirit at work in the groupings historically opposed to their own. This applies both to the oldest Churches in regard to those that left them in protest, and to the newest churches in relation to those from whom they and their forebears came out. In this, the ancient Churches of East and West are more akin to Israel, for they witness to the historic continuity of God's call and promise, passed on from one generation to the next in corporate forms of office and ritual. By contrast, bodies that arose from secession, from charismatic-type irruptions, from protests against decline, are more akin to the initial opening of salvation for the Gentiles who were originally outside the framework of the elect.

This point has important repercussions for Church life and Christian unity. It directly confronts all proprietorial attitudes of Christians, especially Church leaders, towards their traditions. Yes, God has made promises to us; God has covenanted with us, a covenant expressed and embodied in baptism and eucharist. But our election, our gracing, cannot legitimately be used to deny God's grace to others, to outsiders; and it cannot be made a ground for exempting ourselves from divine judgment on our sin.

(3)  Another important principle in Romans 11 is the eventual reunion of those that remained with those who left. This is the clear implication of the promise 'that all Israel will be saved' (Rom 11:26), after 'the full number of the Gentiles [have] come in' (Rom 11:25). This is where Paul's use of *mystery* in verse 25 links up with that in Ephesians, where the mystery of Christ is 'how the Gentiles are fellow heirs [with Israel], members of the same body, and partakers of the promise in Christ Jesus through the gospel' (3:6).

In relation to divisions among Christians, this principle means that God's purpose is always the healing of division and the visible unification of the body of Christ. In the cases where it was truly the Lord's call to separate, never as frequent as seceders claim, the justification for separation is only temporary.

(4)  Romans 11 also hints that the reintegration of Israel may be important for the reunion of separated Gentile Christians. The image of the natural olive tree suggests that a wholly Gentile Christianity was doomed to division. This is implied by Jewish connaturality with the olive tree, which is the one body being formed by the Spirit.

Since the gift and call of God are irrevocable, we should expect that the vocation of Israel to be a priestly people will be restored with their reintegration. In this case, Israel's regrafting into the olive tree will make them mediators of covenant blessing to the Churches of the Gentiles. This perspective reinforces the idea that God will use Israel in the restoration of Christian unity.

Finally, we are to see this astonishing way in which our God uses the repeated disobedience of one grouping for the salvation of others as grounds not for complaint but for an outburst of praise. Paul's astonishment at God's dealings with Israel and the Gentiles lead him to end this remarkable section with one of the most wonderful expressions of praise and amazement before God:

> O the depth of the riches and wisdom and knowledge of God! How unsearchable are his judgments and how inscrutable his ways!
>
> 'For who has known the mind of the Lord,
> or who has been his counsellor?'
> 'Or who has given a gift to him
> that he might be repaid?'
> For from him and through him and to him are all things. To him be glory for ever. Amen. (Rom 11:33–36).

# CHAPTER NINETEEN

# THE PROMISE OF THE SPIRIT AND THE RETURN OF ISRAEL

In the last chapter, we saw that God's promises are without recall. Even our most stubborn disobedience cannot ultimately thwart the purpose of the Lord. Two of the constant promises made by God through the Old Testament prophets concern the gift of the Spirit and the return to the land. The first presents no difficulties to Christians, and the relevant texts are frequently invoked. The second is far more problematic, because the promise of the land raises issues concerning the relationship between Israel and the Church, and the applicability of Old Testament prophecies to contemporary political situations. Recognition that the promises to Israel still stand requires that we examine the promise of the land and whether it has any association with the gift of the Spirit.

The classical passages foretelling the gift of the Spirit are Jeremiah 31:31–34 (on the New Covenant, though it does not actually use the term *ruah*)[1]; Ezekiel 11:19–20; 36:25–29 (promise of the new heart); 37:1–14 (on the vision of the valley of the dry bones). Each passage promising the gift of the indwelling Spirit occurs in a context that also promises the gathering together of the people of Israel and Judah, and their return to the land.[2]

These two themes are so closely intertwined that it is virtually impossible to separate them, especially in Ezekiel. In Ezekiel 36 you have to take very small quotations concerning the Spirit (vv 25–27) if you are not to include the promise about the land (vv 24, 28). These passages suggest that there is a link in the divine plan between the gift of the Spirit and the gathering of the scattered people of Israel with their return to the land. To understand this link requires a closer look at the content of these promises.

## The Spirit and the New Covenant

The following elements are included in the promise:

- God's Law written on the heart (Jer 31:33)
- personal knowledge of God (Jer 31:34; Ezek 37:13)
- forgiveness of sins (Jer 31:34; Ezek 36:25, 29; 37:23)
- gift of a new spirit (Ezek 11:19; 36:26)
- heart of flesh able to obey God (Ezek 11:19–20; 36:26)
- gift of God's own Spirit within (Ezek 36:27; 37:14)
- God's sanctuary will be with them (Ezek 37:28)

Virtually every passage contains the refrain: 'I will be their God, and they shall be my people' (Jer 31:33).[3] This reminds us that the promise of the Spirit in the new covenant is given to the corporate entity of God's people, not primarily to individuals.

## The Promise of the Land

The passages in Jeremiah and Ezekiel that correlate the promise of return with the promise of the new covenant contain the following elements relating to the land:

- exiles brought back from distant countries (Jer 30:10; 31:8, 16, 21; Ezek 11:17; 36:8, 24; 37:12, 14; 37:21)
- enemies punished and destroyed (Jer 30:16,20)
- rebuilding of the ruined cities: Samaria (Jer 30:18; 31:4); Jerusalem (Jer 31:38–39); cities (Ezek 36:11, 33, 35)

- land purged and purified (Ezek 11:18; 36:34)
- age of abundant crops, herds and lavish gifts (Jer 31:12–14, 27; Ezek 36:29–30)
- increase of population (Ezek 36:11, 37)
- end of taunts of the nations (Ezek 36:15)
- Israel and Judah reunited (Ezek 37:19, 22)
- one king to reign over the people (Ezek 37:22, 25).

## The Fulfilment of the Promise

These prophecies were delivered immediately before or during the exile in Babylon. Some have their prime reference in the exile and the return of the exiles:

'Thus says the Lord, the God of Israel: Like these good figs, so I will regard as good the exiles from Judah, whom I have sent away from this place to the land of the Chaldeans. I will set my eyes upon them for good, and I will bring them back to this land. I will build them up, and not tear them down; I will plant them, and not uproot them.' (Jer 24:5–6)

With all these prophecies of restoration, there was a first level of fulfilment in the return from the exile, and the rebuilding of the temple and the Holy City of Jerusalem. But the language and vision of the prophets far exceeded the limited scope of the post-exilic restoration under Zerubbabel and Joshua the priest. The return only affected Judah, not Israel; it did not involve the restoration of the monarchy and the rule of the 'one king . . . David, my servant'; (Ezek 36:30). Most importantly the full promise of the Spirit remains a hope for the Messianic future, even though the post-exilic restoration saw a degree of spiritual revival.

Many details point to the Messianic character of the promise. The references to the Davidic king (Ezek 37:24–25) link up with the Messianic promises of Isaiah (Isa 9:6–7; 11:1). Jeremiah links the Davidic line with the return to the land (23:5–8; 33:15–16). Further, the return to the land is closely linked to knowledge that Yahweh is the Lord (Ezek 36:11, 38; 37:14). In two places he states the nations will know that Yahweh is the Lord (Ezek 36:23; 37:28). These are functions elsewhere attributed to the coming Messiah (Isa 7:15; 9:7; 11:1–5).

Christians have always seen the fulfilment of Old Testament prophecy in the coming of God's Son in the Incarnation. It is the eternal Son of God made flesh who forgives sins, who gives the indwelling Spirit, who writes the new law on believers' hearts, who reveals the knowledge of God. The historic Christian tradition of East and West has instinctively rejected any interpretation of the Old Testament promises that by-passes Christ, for example by seeing partial fulfilment in Jesus' first coming and partial fulfilment elsewhere. It sees 'the day of the Lord' with the execution of God's judgment on the world as realized in the 'hour' of Jesus. In particular, Christians have seen the promise of the Spirit and the new covenant fulfilled in the outpouring of the Holy Spirit at Pentecost. This connection is explicitly made in Hebrews 8:8–12, which quotes Jeremiah 31:31–34 and relates this promise to the ministry of Jesus: 'But as it is, Christ has obtained a ministry which is as much more excellent than the old as the covenant he mediates is better, since it is enacted on better promises' (Heb 8:6).

## Christian Answers to Apparent Partial Fulfilment

The major way the Christians interpreted the fulfilment of the promises of the Old Testament was to spiritualize them. The Christian Church is seen as the heir of the promises, and becomes the new Israel. But whereas the old covenant promised earthly blessings, the new brings spiritual blessings in heaven. This is the schema in the letter to the Hebrews, but also characterizes the teaching of Paul, e.g. in 1 Corinthians 10 and 2 Corinthians 3. The promises concerning Jerusalem are fulfilled in the heavenly Jerusalem, while the earthly Jerusalem is in slavery with her children (Gal 4:25–26). The abundance of crops and livestock promised to the faithful in the old covenant is realized in the spiritual abundance of the new People of God, upon whom the Spirit of Pentecost has come.

A second strand in the Christian explanation lay in the conviction that the Lord who came in human weakness will return in glory. In this way, promises concerning the Messiah are truly fulfilled in Jesus, but their full reality will only be achieved and manifested in Jesus' second coming. This explanation can be seen in New Testament prophecy, as in Revelation 21:3–4, which picks up and reshapes the promises of Isaiah 25:7–8 and 35:10.[4] The return of the Lord inaugurates a new heaven and a new earth. The complete fulfilment will not just be in a fellowship of spirits, but will involve a spiritualized material cosmos.

Thus in the New Testament, the promises interpreted spiritually are eschatological. While wars and mourning are not ended and the wolf is not yet dwelling with the lamb, the resurrection of Jesus is understood as the first fruits of the resurrection of the entire human race. It is in the final resurrection that all the promises will be fulfilled. The risen and ascended Jesus already embodies their total fulfilment, 'having received from the Father the promise of the Holy Spirit' (Acts 2:33). The rest is to come, but what is to come will be the unfolding of what is already realized in the glorified physical Christ in heaven.

The realization in Jesus also has application to the land. It was the function of Israel to prepare for the Messiah, to give birth to the Holy One of God. Here the people and the land are inseparable.[5] The whole reality of Israel which includes its physical dwelling-place shapes and brings forth its intended fruit in Jesus. We can sense this link in the words of Isaiah: 'In that day the branch of the Lord shall be beautiful and glorious, and the fruit of the land shall be the pride and glory of the survivors of Israel' (4:2). There is a connection between the branch of the Lord and the fruit of the land. Both are realized in Jesus himself.

## Recovering Our Full Heritage

When we examine the extraordinary richness of the Old Testament promise and its New Testament fulfilment, we can sense that many Churches today are weak in proclaiming this richness. Many fundamentalists and conservative evangelicals deserve credit for taking the details of Old Testament prophecy seriously. However, the widespread adoption of a dispensationalist schema has resulted in the separation of the destiny of Israel from that of the Christian Church, and thus a failure to hold together the two covenants. This separation unintentionally diminishes the centrality of Christ. However, they are right to protest against a situation in which the return of the Lord and divine judgment are rarely mentioned and Church hopes are focused excessively on this world.

The root problem is the dichotomy between the physical and the spiritual. Centuries of a wrong kind of spiritualization have led to life after death being seen individualistically in terms of the immortality of the soul rather than the general resurrection of the dead. This trend weakens understanding of *signs* in the biblical sense, in which the immediate physical reality mediates and makes present the deeper spiritual reality to which it points and which it embodies. As a result, 'spiritual' people are less interested in the physical and sensory. The earth and the cosmos are reduced to temporary habitats of no lasting significance, the body a shell to be discarded.

It is then highly significant that the baptism in the Holy Spirit both reawakens hope in the second coming of Jesus and has a distinctively physical dimension. The Pentecostal and charismatic movements represent a massive counter-thrust of the Spirit against every tendency to marginalize the physical. The fact that Pentecostal and charismatic Christians tend not to be satisfied with

mere spiritualization of the promise of the land to Israel
may not be merely a manifestation of fundamentalism.
It stems from a deep sense that the sending of the Holy
Spirit penetrates matter, raises up the sick and lifeless
body, and manifests the glory of the Lord in redeemed,
restored creation.

However, the promises to Israel have to be understood
in a Christocentric framework in which the higher-level
heavenly fulfilment of the old covenant is firmly upheld.
In this light, we should see the promises concerning
the land as being fulfilled eschatologically: their total
fulfilment will be in the new land at the centre of the new
earth, upon which the new Jerusalem will come down 'out
of heaven from God, prepared as a bride adorned for her
husband' (Rev 21:2). The fulfilment of the promise of the
land will involve all the prophets foretold, the knowledge
of God, total cleansing from sin, the full indwelling of
the Holy Spirit, the end of all pain and tribulations.
While it will be a resurrection-existence in which the
spirit permeates and suffuses the physical, it will be
a more earthly reality than Christians have commonly
imagined.

In this light, the return of Israel to the land of Palestine
is more significant than mainline Christians have generally recognized, but significant in a different way from
what many fundamentalists proclaim. It is truly an
affirmation of the enduring validity of the promises to
Israel, but it is still a sign and harbinger of the future
fulfilment at the second coming.

In this context we can see a correlation between the
return of Israel to the land and the rise of Messianic
Judaism. For the reappearance of a distinctively Jewish
Christianity is itself a sign of the coming fulfilment of
Paul's affirmation that 'all Israel will be saved' (Rom
11:26). Israel's return to the land cannot be separated
from Israel's acceptance of the full revelation of the God
who is the Father of our Lord Jesus Christ. Messianic
Judaism represents the first time, since the early Christian
generations, that Jews are able to accept Jesus as Messiah
without abandoning or diminishing their Jewishness.

Since all Israel will be saved, and this salvation belongs to the period of history ending with the second coming, the promises concerning the Spirit and the land will have a this-worldly realization. But this is not the sole meaning of these promises, which relate both to the first coming, especially Jesus' ascension into heaven, and to the second coming, with the establishment of the new heaven and the new earth.

## Summary

These reflections lead to a schema on these lines:

(1)  there is a degree of fulfilment of the Old Testament promises in the Incarnation and Jesus' earthly ministry;

(2)  there is a complete realization in the resurrection–ascension of Jesus Christ, which is a fulfilment in the heavenlies;

(3)  there will be a degree of fulfilment of the promises to Israel in this age with a people restored to the land accepting Jesus as the Messiah;

(4)  there is a partial fulfilment in the Church on earth, through the gift of the Spirit that is a first-fruits (*aparché*) and pledge-guarantee (*arrabón*) of the fulness to come;

(5)  however, the final fulfilment of both the promise of the Spirit and of the land will be realized in the new heaven and the new earth, when the holy city, the new Jerusalem, comes down out of heaven from God, prepared as a bride adorned for her husband (Rev 21:2).

# PART III

## Return to the Present

# CHAPTER TWENTY

# RECONCILIATION AND REINTEGRATION IN CHRIST

W e can now try to pull together some of the strands already uncovered. In particular, we can look at the over-all significance of the following elements:

(1)   God always acts in view of the end God had in view from before creation. The particular are chosen for the sake of all, so that the chosen are a priestly people (Chapter 13).

(2)   The promises and the threats are given to the same people of God. The promises following disaster are of the rebuilding and restoration of Zion, of the reunification of Judah and Israel, and of return to their inheritance (Chapter 14).

(3)   The progression of the Spirit's outpouring in the twentieth century is in some way the inverse of the spread of the Church from the initial outpouring at Pentecost. In the origins there was a move outward from Judaism, and in the present there is a move from the diaspora towards the historic centre and roots (Chapter 3).

## From the Physical to the Spiritual

Israel holds the key to Christian unity. This follows from God's decision to establish the Christian Church on the foundation of the people of the old covenant. Israel is called to prepare for the Messiah, and from the tribe of Judah comes the root that gives birth to the Son of God. So the Messiah is depicted as a branch, a stem or a fruit growing out of Israel: 'There shall come forth a shoot from the stump of Jesse, and a branch shall grow out of his roots' (Isa 11:1).[1]

In this process of Church-formation, God calls a people as the matrix for the elevation of humankind to the dignity of sons and daughters of the Father. This elevation occurs through a process of divine call and divine intervention, in which the eternal plan of God directed towards the only begotten Son, the 'first-born of all creation' (Col 1:15) is unfolded and unveiled. From the call of Abraham and the covenant sealed in circumcision, there is a steady progression through the exodus from Egypt, the covenant of Sinai and the giving of the law, the entry into the promised land, the establishment of the Davidic kingdom, the election of Jerusalem, the call of the prophets, the increasing Messianic hope, the first intimations of resurrection and of heavenly existence. All these prepare for the incarnation of the Son of God, the inauguration of the eschatological kingdom and the outpouring of the Spirit on the sons and daughters of the Father. In this process, we can note two fundamental principles of God's ways:

(1) *God moves from the earthly to the heavenly, from the physical-material to the spiritual*: This order from the lower to the higher is expressed in the first creation account in Genesis 1, where only at the climax of the six days of creation does God create man and woman 'in his own image' (Gen 1:27). It is implicit in all typology, in which a preparatory reality in the Old Testament points to and teaches something about the New Testament fulfilment in Jesus Christ.

(2) *In this process, God builds each new stage on those that he had previously established. God never leaves the starting-point behind*. The raising to the heavenly-spiritual level does not abandon the earthly-physical. Over a period of two thousand years God acts to shape a people for God's own, elevating the faithful children of Abraham to be the human ancestry of the Christ (see Rom 9:4–5).

It is in the context of his teaching on the resurrection of the body that Paul formulates a kind of principle that would seem to have much wider application: 'It is not the spiritual which is first but the physical, and then the spiritual' (1 Cor 15:46). This statement directly addressed the objection that resurrection of the body was a notion unworthy of truly spiritual people. So Paul explains in words hard for us to understand: 'It is sown a physical body, it is raised a spiritual body' (1 Cor 15:44). Paul is pointing to the climax of the whole history of salvation, which will involve, not the end of the body and the physical creation, but the resurrection of the body and the creation of a new heaven and a new earth, in which the spiritual will totally suffuse and transform the physical.

Part of this divine process of raising up the spiritual within the physical is a development in the pattern of divine interventions. As salvation history unfolds, God's transforming activity within and on humanity does not diminish; rather the fruits of the interventions are ever deeper. This spiritual elevation is at the same time a deeper entry of God into this material world. This process reaches its climax in the Incarnation, in which the eternal Word literally becomes flesh (John 1:14).

While signs and wonders accompany the preaching of the gospel, for Jesus the only sign to be given is 'the sign of Jonah' (Matt 16:4). The two greatest interventions of God in the fulfilment of the Messianic promises are the conception of the Son of God and his resurrection from the dead, both of which occur out of human sight. This does not diminish the element of manifestation; thus Jesus' coming is spoken of as an 'appearing' (2 Tim 1:10), but the deep reality of what has become visible is only seen by the eyes of faith (see also 1 John 1:1–3).

The story of Pentecost is a paradigm for the experience of the Church. The coming of the Spirit is described as an event whose transforming power is primarily interior and most evident to the recipients. It is neither invisible to others, nor outwardly dazzling; the visible effects cause reactions ranging from amazement to ridicule. The most significant effects are the changed lives of the disciples, leading to their bold and confident proclamation of the gospel.

Similarly, the miracles performed by Jesus are never melodramatic, and they are reported with remarkable sobriety. These factors accord with Jesus' own insistence that the works of power are never ends in themselves, but point to the divine life he has come to give.

Thus the process from the physical to the spiritual involves a deepening in the patterns of divine intervention and a deepening in the human response of faith. It is the logic of the remnant and of the self-emptying that divine power is shown in the midst of human weakness. So the Lord tells Paul: 'My grace is sufficient for you, for my power is made perfect in weakness' (2 Cor 12:9).

Signs and wonders do belong to the period of the Church, but they do not exempt charismatic Christians from the conditions of servanthood and of weakness. In this age, 'our knowledge is imperfect' (1 Cor 13:9) and we know only 'in part' (1 Cor 13:12).

## Israel, the Christ and the Church

These principles are of immense relevance for the relationship between the two covenants, and between Israel and the Church. The physical comes first – that is Israel according to the flesh. The hall-mark of this covenant is the physical sign of circumcision. The preparation of Israel for the coming of the Christ involves an elevation so that Israel can bring forth a Son to be filled with the Spirit of God; so we see in the Old Testament a purification and raising up of the remnant who are the beginnings of Israel according to the Spirit. We see this reality clearly present in the infancy gospel of Luke which notes so insistently the role of the Holy Spirit in the lives of Zechariah and Elizabeth, of Joseph and Mary, of Simeon and Anna.

The Church in gestation reaches a new stage with the conception and birth of Jesus Christ. This birth is only possible by the power of the Holy Spirit. Having a human mother but no human father presents the two key elements that recur throughout the formation of the

Church: (a) the Christ is formed from pre-existent human material – through his mother, and is thus part of human history and of Israel; (b) the Christ is not of this world, but comes from the Father, and is born 'of God' (John 1:13).

In the earthly Christ, the Spirit is present and operative, but by divine purpose is limited in the conditions of alienated humanity. The Church is embodied in Christ, who becomes the 'life-giving Spirit' in his resurrection, when all limitations to the working of the Spirit in Jesus are removed. His humanity is totally penetrated with the Spirit of God and becomes the instrument of the Father to bring the Church to birth and maturity.

## Consequences for Christian Unity

Because the physical comes first, but is not left behind, the Church is born from the physical Israel (human mother) and from the sovereign intervention of the Spirit (divine paternity). So for the Fathers of the Church the Church is born from the side of Christ on the cross – through the instrumentality of his humanity and the power of the Holy Spirit. Likewise, at Pentecost, the Church is formed out of Jewish flesh confessing Christ and enlivened by the gift of the Spirit from heaven.

Thus the Church in God's plan is the ingrafting of the Gentiles into the body of Jewish believers in the Messiah. So the letter to the Ephesians presents the nature of the Church as the reconciliation of Jews and Gentiles, with the Gentiles being made 'fellow heirs, members of the same body, and partakers of the promise in Christ Jesus through the gospel' (Eph 3:6). From this perspective, there is something unbalanced, literally uncatholic, about a wholly Gentile Church, or a Church in which Jewish converts have been totally assimilated into Gentile culture.

It is no coincidence that the most earthly and physical Churches are the ancient Churches of East and West, the Orthodox and the Catholic. They may appear to Protestant Christians to be less spiritual, but the earthiness of their sacramental forms is the result of direct descent from the Church's Jewish roots. This does not mean that the ancient Churches cannot suffer grave spiritual decline, but that the deeply embodied forms of Catholic and Orthodox worship are not inherently an argument against their spiritual character, indeed rather the opposite.

In fact, only material-physical beings can form a body. It is the characteristic of the Church as the body of Christ to represent the harmonization of many physical members through the work of the one Spirit from which they drink. Angels cannot and do not form community, as Thomas Aquinas remarked.

Protestant Christianity represents a protest for truth (the Word) against a debased Christianity, in which outward forms were no longer experienced as the bearers of gospel truth. But as the history of Protestantism demonstrates, organic unity is impossible on the basis of the written Word alone, apart from reconciliation with the historic roots from which the faith has come. Pentecostalism represents a protest for Spirit against a powerless and largely cerebral Protestantism, in which attachment to the Word was not evidently accompanied by the vitality of the Spirit. While the Spirit of God brings the Word to life, the history of the Pentecostal movement illustrates that Spirit and Word need something more to produce the unity of the body of Christ. That more is the original body and the original flesh: the ancient Churches of East and West, and, most importantly, Israel.

## The Pattern of Christian Unity

The work of Jesus is to gather all God's people into one (John 11:52). He is himself the 'one new man' making peace between Jew and Gentile, reconciling 'both to God in one body through the cross' (Eph 2:15–16). The fulness of Jesus' reconciling work requires the reconciliation of Jew and Gentile in the one body of Christ, the healing of all Christian divisions and the evangelization of the unconverted.

The order of surprises of the Spirit in the Pentecostal

and charismatic movements may well indicate the strategy and order of the Lord in this process of ecumenical reconciliation. This represents a somewhat different historical schema from the 'full gospel' view popular among Pentecostals: original apostolic fullness and power, then drastic decline through centuries of darkness, followed by phases of restoration: the gospel of justification by faith through Luther, sanctification through Wesley and the Holiness movement, and the 'full gospel' of baptism in the Spirit and the spiritual gifts in the Pentecostal movement.[2] This schema was fashioned in a separatist atmosphere in which each new wave comes out from its parent Church to form a new body or movement of the enlightened. Neither Martin Luther nor John Wesley would have subscribed to any schema of this kind.

The order of the surprises from the Pentecostal back through the classical Protestant to the Roman Catholic and the Jewish represents an order of reconciliation and reintegration. This unfolding order manifests a profound logic of the Spirit. In this process, the Pentecostals stand for life and power, the Protestants for gospel principle, the Catholics (and Orthodox) for organic substance,[3] the Jews for the flesh, that is, for bodily corporate historical roots.

In this sequence, the Pentecostal movement represents the power and vitality of the Holy Spirit of God. It represents a recovery of the Lordship of the Trinity over both the Church and the written Word. Certainly the Spirit needs both the Church and the Word, but their roles are to be instruments of the Spirit. The primary Protestant contribution is in the area of principle. The Protestant principles were originally elaborated in the face of widespread corruption and superstition in the Church; the doctrines of the atonement and of salvation by Christ, the unique authority of the Word of God, and justification by faith, together safeguard the uniqueness of Christ, of the Scriptures and of trusting faith (*fiducia*).

Principles can govern the life of a body, but they cannot construct a body. The Protestant principles require application in the organic historical body of Christ. In other words, movements of spiritual protest against the corruption and degeneration of Christian forms must eventually achieve reconciliation with the embodied forms against whose debasement the protests were made. Catholic substance represents the truth that Catholicism (and Orthodoxy) are not simply a set of principles, but are of their nature organic bodies with the full range of components that form a living body (on the analogy of joints, tissue, bones and blood). As such, they have a continuous history from the Church's apostolic origins.

It is significant that the Pentecostal movement has involved, in practice though not in doctrine, a recovery of physical elements traditionally ignored in the Protestant Churches: laying on of hands in ministry, bodily expression in worship, dance, the physicality of tongues, emphasis on bodily healing. In this respect, Pentecostalism represents not simply a further distancing from the origins, but a return towards embodied incarnate Christianity. It is no coincidence that this more embodied celebration of life in the charismatic renewal found easier acceptance in the more liturgical traditions of historic Christianity.[4]

## Models for Unity

The bringing together of separated Christian Churches is more complex than the reconciliation of Judah and Israel. For the different Christian bodies are not the same kind of entity. The Pentecostals (and some of their immediate predecessors), in effect represent revival movements that in the process of taking on structural forms have fragmented into denominations. The main Reformation Churches (Lutheran, Reformed, Mennonite) are principle Churches, founded on certain doctrinal principles. Churches which represent national schisms from Western Catholicism (Anglican, Scandinavian Lutheran) retain greater elements of Catholic substance.

In this situation, reintegration has to be on the basis of the work of the Holy Spirit in each grouping and tradition, which means respecting its original character in its positive witness. The root problem seems to be how to integrate revivals, principles and organic substance. The history of the ecumenical movement suggests that any kind of ecclesiastical democracy that treats all the divided Churches as equal partners is doomed to frustration. Very different and unequal partners need to take each other with equal seriousness and treat each other with equal respect, which is a different matter. Only the Spirit of God can reveal the way through this minefield. But a few points can be usefully made.

First, there would appear to be a trinitarian pattern in the divisions in the West. The Pentecostals emphasize the life of the Spirit, the Protestants the truth of the Word, and the Catholics the organic substance of the faith from its origins in the Father. This perspective confirms the recent ecumenical emphasis on the importance of communion (*koinonia*).

Secondly, this schema suggests the greatest onus is on the Roman Catholic Church. Ultimately, reintegration is impossible without the historic Church in communion with Rome being seen convincingly to be the Church of the Word and the Church of the Spirit. The Catholic Church already includes within its communion, groupings whose origins represented a stand for principle against worldliness and corruption (monasticism and monastic reforms, the mendicant friars, the Society of Jesus), and has welcomed currents of revival associated with charismatic preachers (St Anthony of Padua, St Bernardine, St Vincent Ferrer).

Thirdly, the Pentecostal witness to the Spirit of life and power has to be anchored in the process of enfleshment and interiorization. It will be unable to make its distinctive contribution to Christian unity and fulness if it takes as its model earlier Old Testament patterns of material blessing and prosperity, or if it makes the parallel mistake of emphasizing the extraordinary and the external in the manifestation of the Spirit.

Fourthly, what we may call the anthropological components in Christian divisions (Pentecostal emphasis on spirit, Protestant emphasis on Word and truth, Catholic

emphasis on continuity and body) corroborate the importance of Judaism for the reunion of separated Christians.
For Israel and then Judaism saw an evolution from what
was very bodily (a people formed by physical deliverance
and marked by the bodily sign of circumcision) to a formation by Word (especially through the prophets) to an
understanding of Spirit (in the wisdom and apocalyptic
literature). But in this process, the spiritual never lost
touch with the bodily. So the antitheses modern Western
Christians inherit, between outer and inner, between rite
and spirit, are – despite occasional prophetic protests –
quite foreign to the Scriptures of both Testaments.

Messianic Judaism has in its short life already developed sufficiently to indicate that it is likely to strain the
received evangelical Protestant framework within which
it arose. The Messianic Jews are instinctively liturgical.
They naturally adopt a form of biblical fidelity which is
not afraid of ritual and outward forms. It is therefore
of vital importance for the proper contribution of Messianic Judaism to Christian unity that Gentile Christians,
whether Catholic or Protestant, give them the space to
develop in fidelity to the Spirit and to make their unique
contribution to Catholic–Protestant reconciliation.

# CHAPTER TWENTY-ONE

# COME, LORD JESUS

G rasping the importance of the role of Israel in the restoration of Christian unity prepares us to re-examine the second coming of Jesus. It was noted in Chapter Seven that revival movements manifesting the spiritual gifts have been particularly marked by a heightened eschatological hope.

## The Church and the Parousia

The coming of the Holy Spirit kindles the Church's hope. 'May the God of hope fill you with all joy and peace in believing, so that by the power of the Holy Spirit you may abound in hope' (Rom 15:13). A lifeless Church may have many plans, but it will have little hope. In the New Testament we can see how central the hope in Jesus' return was in the Christian consciousness. The Parousia was central to early Christian faith to a degree that it is almost impossible for contemporary Christians to realize.

Sometimes people dismiss this prominence by attributing it to a mistaken assumption of the Lord's early return. However, this eschatological hope was a direct extension and intensification of the Jewish hope for the coming of the Messiah. In the synoptics, Jesus' message develops from the coming of the kingdom associated with his own person, to the return of the Son of Man to inaugurate the final reign at the end of the ages. As the first Christians came to understand that God's saving purpose would be achieved through two comings of the Messiah rather than one (see the response in Acts 1:11b to the question of Acts 1:6), the longing for total salvation at the heart of Messianic faith was redirected to the promised second coming.

For the first Christians, it was of the nature of the Church to long for the Parousia. It is the longing of the Lord and the longing of the Church. The Spirit and the Bride say, "Come," both to the believer and to the Lord. 'And let him who hears say, "Come."' (Rev 22:17). The Spirit instructs the Bride, the one 'who hears', on how to say 'Come'.

Jesus instructs his disciples:

> Let your loins be girded and your lamps burning, and be like men who are waiting for their master to come home from the marriage feast, so that they may open to him at once when he comes and knocks. Blessed are those servants whom the master finds awake when he comes; truly, I say to you, he will gird himself and have them sit at table, and he will come and serve them. If he comes in the second watch, or in the third, and finds them so, blessed are those servants! (Luke 12:35–38)

In Jesus' mind, to be prepared for the master's return is of the essence of faithful discipleship. It reveals the fully personal character of Christian life, for the Christian is not just expecting an event, but awaiting the return of the Beloved Master. The person however is not separated from the work. The return of the King will bring the realization of the kingdom, and what numerous New Testament references simply term *salvation* (1 Thess 5:8; 2 Tim 2:10; Heb 1:14; 1 Pet 1:5), full and final deliverance from Satan, sin, evil and death.

A focus on the second coming is the proper accompaniment to a zeal for evangelism. In Matthew's gospel we are told: 'This gospel of the kingdom will be preached throughout the whole world, as a testimony to all nations; and then the end will come' (Matt 24:14). The Spirit that evokes a longing for the return of Jesus impels us to go out into all the world to proclaim the gospel of the kingdom.

We want to preach this word of life because we desire all people to be saved and because we long for our Lord to be manifested in all his glory.

It is the calling of the Church to proclaim this hope and to be the faithful people who pray for its realization. By the gift of the Spirit, the Church that is the body of Christ already anticipates in this world the eternal kingdom to come. So the Church not only proclaims the return of her Lord, but witnesses by her divine life to the reality of the coming kingdom.

## The Effects of Prayer for the Parousia

It is perhaps in the area of eschatological hope that there is the biggest gap between what Church liturgies proclaim and the personal convictions of participants. All the ancient Christian liturgies are impregnated with faith in the second coming of Jesus and a longing for that final fulfilment. At every eucharist, Roman Catholics say 'Amen' to the words 'as we wait in joyful hope for the coming of our Saviour, Jesus Christ'.[1] But there is not much evidence that the Christian people are in fact expecting and hoping for this climactic event. More often their hope is heaven after death, understood in an individualistic framework.

Chapter Seven noted that one effect of baptism in the Spirit is the awakening of this eschatological hope. As the reality of the risen and ascended Jesus is established within the Christian, the longing for his return is enkindled. As Christians pray for the second coming, this prayer changes them and changes the Church. Praying for the Parousia is the most effective and radical way of challenging the earthly establishment of the Church. Earthly establishment refers to all the ways of thinking and acting that assume, maybe unconsciously, that the Church naturally belongs to this world and finds its proper home in this world.

This prayer for the second coming will lead the Churches into the saving judgment of God. It holds the key to radical renewal of faith, for it confronts the Churches with

the Sovereign Lord of history. It makes plain the servant
role of the Church, exposing all the ways in which the
servant has exalted herself rather than her Lord. Before
Almighty God and the Son, made the judge of the living
and of the dead, the Church's true character and role
is revealed. Jesus' many parables and teachings on the
master's return and the judgment constantly emphasize
the test of true servants.

This prayer will lead Christians to see the 'Our Father'
in a new light. For the Lord's prayer is strongly eschatological. It is an indication of our loss of authentic
Christian hope that we pray the Our Father without
conscious eschatological reference. 'Thy kingdom come'
is praying for the complete effecting of God's purpose.
'Thy will be done on earth as it is in heaven', will be
fully realized only with the establishment of the new
heaven and the new earth. 'Lead us not into temptation
(trial)' and 'Deliver us from evil (the evil one)' have strong
tones of prayer for protection and deliverance in the final
battle.

## The Parousia and Orthodox Faith

Prayer for the Parousia, expressing a revitalized eschatological hope, is the surest way to safeguard and promote
full orthodoxy of Christian faith. This may seem a strange
statement in view of the common association between
fascination with the end-times and wild vagaries of
belief. But while speculation about the timing and the
schedule of the final act is frequently linked to oddity,
simple prayer for the Lord's return is another matter.

This prayer affirms all the essential points of the
Church's creed. It is Trinitarian, because it is the Son
who returns to complete the mission from the Father,
and this prayer can only be kindled by the indwelling
Spirit of God. It is strongly incarnational, because it is
as incarnate Son, the God-man, that he returns, coming
back to his own to complete the divine work of bodily
resurrection. It is necessarily ecclesial and corporate, for
the Parousia is the Lord's return for the final gathering

of his people. This prayer will set in proper order the relationships between the Church on earth and the Church of glory, bringing those who pray it into a deeper grasp of the sacramental and veiled presence of the heavenly in the earthly. It will clarify the proper role of Word and sacrament: the Word that proclaims the age to come in the midst of this world, and the sacrament that embodies in sign form the holy realities of the coming kingdom.

## The Parousia and Christian Unity

The Parousia as object of Christian hope plays an essential role in the quest for Christian unity. It is the official confession of every Christian body. All Christians pray 'Thy kingdom come'. All Christians ought therefore to be united in praying the final prayer of the Scriptures 'Amen. Come, Lord Jesus!' (Rev 22:20).

Such a united prayer *Maranatha* is intimately linked with the John chapter 17 prayer for Christian unity taught by the Abbé Couturier of Lyon, France. Couturier saw that the only prayer for unity that all Christians could fully share is the prayer of Jesus himself that 'they may all be one; even as thou, Father, art in me, and I in thee' (John 17:21). He thus developed this form of prayer for Christian unity 'in the form that Christ wills and by the means that he wills'. The perspective of this chapter adds to Couturier's vision a greater emphasis on the role of the Holy Spirit and a stronger eschatology. The prayer for unity, inviting Jesus to pray his prayer in us that all may be one as he and the Father are one, has to be a prayer in the power of the Spirit. The Spirit's prayer that Christians be one and the Spirit's cry 'Come, Lord Jesus' are closely related, for the second coming will be the final gathering into the full unity of the kingdom.

This association naturally raises the question as to whether Christians should expect the re-establishment of Christian unity before the Lord's return. While the full transformation will only come with the Parousia, there are strong grounds for believing that there will be significant reconciliation before then. First of all, the

effective evangelization of the world requires the witness
of unity among Christians for which Jesus prayed (John
17:20–21). We might also ask ourselves two questions:
(a) Is it conceivable that Jesus could return without
the Jewish people having turned to their Messiah? (b)
Is it conceivable that Jesus could return and find all the
different Churches as divided as they are at present?

In Romans, Paul indicates that the end cannot come
until the hardening [in part] of Israel has come to an
end. In God's plan the destiny of the nations and that of
Israel are inextricably bound together (Rom 11:25–32).
The affirmation that 'all Israel will be saved' (Rom
11:26) implies that the Jewish people will accept the
Messiah before the Lord's return. Because of the close
connection between Israel and the nature of the Church,
it is unthinkable that the Messianic completion of Jewish
faith would have no repercussions on the relationships
between divided Christians.

But a more fundamental reason flows from the nature
of the Church as the 'one new man' formed from Jew and
Gentile. A de-judaized Church has a weakened knowledge
of Jesus as Messiah and Lord. The conversion of the Jews
and the reunion of Jew and Gentile in the one body will
have enormous effects on our grasp of Scripture, and
our understanding of the Messiah and Lord who is its
centre. Only a Church renewed through the reintegration
of Israel can be a Church properly disposed to welcome
and recognize the returning Master.

The Scriptures depict the Church on earth as a waiting
people, ardently awaiting the return of the bridegroom.
This expectation calls for a unity and fellowship in the
wait. The full welcome of the returning Lord requires
a common joy among the fellow-welcomers. As long as
Christians revile and exclude other Christians, they are
not ready to welcome the Lord who acknowledges all who
confess his name and keep his commandments.

# CHAPTER TWENTY-TWO

# BACK TO THE NON-DENOMINATIONALS

Now that we have seen the complementarity of Jew and Gentile in God's plan, and sensed more of the paradoxical unity of election and rejection, we are in a better position to reconsider the significance of non-denominational charismatic Christianity. If God has bound all over to disobedience in order to have mercy on all (Rom 11:32), then we are to understand the paradox of concurrent charismatic renewal in the mainline Christian Churches and a massive outpouring of Spirit-life outside these Churches in the light of human disobedience and divine mercy.

The series of divine surprises – this outpouring of the Holy Spirit on the Pentecostals, on classical Protestants, on Roman Catholics and on Messianic Jews – demonstrates both the intensity of the Lord's determination to save all people and the faithfulness of the Lord to all the Churches and traditions that bear and confess the name of Christ. This series manifests the Lord's deep desire to gather all the redeemed into one.

The abundant outpouring of God's Spirit among the independent charismatics does not fit immediately into this pattern of reconciliation and reintegration. It speaks rather to the degree of disobedience in the mainline Churches. It is not for any of us to judge each other. But whenever new streams of spiritual vitality and dynamism spring up outside our systems, we have to suspect that our disobedience and our resistance to the Lord are greater than we realize. For it is because of hardness of heart, because of resistance to God's ways and to God's gifts, among those officially dedicated to the message and the life of Christ, that the Lord has his way elsewhere. So deep is the divine determination to save the lost, to raise up sons and daughters to radiate the life of the Spirit, that the Lord will do outside the historic framework what is resisted inside. Those of us within the older Church traditions are invited to reflect on the reply of John the Baptist to those Jews who prided themselves on their lineage: 'I tell you that out of these stones God can raise up children for Abraham' (Matt 3:9 NIV). When the established Churches are not fully open to the work of the Spirit, who can tell the Lord not to pour out the Spirit elsewhere? The promise of the Lord is not to restrict the gift to those originally chosen, but that they as a people will not be abandoned.

It is in this light that we can interpret much of the history of modern Evangelicalism, Pentecostalism and now charismatic independency. Since the beginnings of Evangelicalism in the 1730s there has been a growing dichotomy between institution and life, between outer and inner, between Church and evangelism. In many respects, the development of the Holiness movement in the late 19th century, the rise of Pentecostalism in the early 20th century, and the explosion of charismatic independency since the 1970s represent a steady intensification of this dichotomy. There is in this different series of developments a steady increase in life and blessings outside the received structures. With the Pentecostal movement comes the Pentecostal gift of the Spirit, the full range of spiritual gifts, the release of praise, and the enlivening and empowering of every believer. With this too came a whole recovery of physical forms of worship and ministry that point to the original vitality of the sacramental signs cherished in the liturgical Churches. With the non-denominational explosion comes, in many circles, a stronger sense of the corporate character of the Spirit's work, and of the range of ministries given to impact the world and drive back the inroads of evil. With this latest move outside the historic structures, there is a clear vision and a spiritual power for the establishment of vibrant local churches.

The inter-locking of God's judgment and God's mercy should lead all parties who confess the name of Christ to a humility before the Lord. God's forbearance towards the historic expressions of the Church is much greater than any of us imagine. But in pouring out grace and life in places that we would not expect, God shows an amazing willingness to shower blessings upon believers who may be far from the sanctity and the wisdom of mature Christians. Our God is a God who has taken the risk of Incarnation. Every gift of grace is a similar risk. God does not compel sons and daughters born of the Spirit, and is not niggardly with the gift of divine life. The signs of the Spirit's presence are not proofs of anything except God's reckless generosity and the seriousness of God's purpose – and an openness in the recipients.

## The Challenge to the Mainline Churches

Each new step in God's bestowal of life and gifts outside the received structures poses a bigger problem and challenge for all those Christians deeply convinced of the historic embodiment of Christian faith passed down from generation to generation within a succession of faith and of ministerial office. The very idea of 'new churches' is inconceivable for many Catholics and Orthodox, for whom the structures of church worship and ministry flow directly from the historic Jesus into the apostolic Church. There is an essential link between the divine–human union in the person of Christ, and the divine–human union in the mystery of the Church, which is his body. In this light, the newest wave of multiplying independent churches is easily seen as the latest manifestation of a misguided sectarianism and of a self-confident modernity uninterested in historical roots.

The biggest hurdle to overcome is the fear of looking at the facts and of having to modify noble assumptions about the faith, the Church and our Christian identity. It is the challenge posed by every intervention of God in the power of the Spirit, supremely in the Incarnation. To meet and to know personally many of the leaders in the new independent churches is often to be impressed by their dedication to Jesus Christ and the signs of the Holy Spirit in their lives and ministries. It is also to become aware of the immense pressures that numerical 'success' can bring in its wake.

Once this leap of recognition has been made, the perspective opened up by our reflection, especially on Romans 9–11, suggests that this intensification of 'extra-ordinary' blessings should be received by the mainline Churches as an invitation to self-examination and to repentance.[1] We should ask: What is this life that is being given to these 'outsiders'? Why is the life of the Spirit being manifested more clearly in many of these new churches than among ourselves? What in our own Church prevents the Lord from doing the same among us?' As we ask these questions, the Lord will humble us and open the way for deeper renewal in our own Church. Possibly the encounter with the new independent churches will show more clearly than anything else the seriousness of the condition of our Churches and the depth of repentance and renewal required.

It can be salutary to know how the new church people often see the older Churches. The general picture they see is of dwindling and ageing congregations, that have no visible impact on surrounding society, that do not evan-gelize, whose members do not love one another, that are resistant to change, that uphold a view of themselves and their importance that is not borne out by visible evidence. While this is clearly not the whole picture, it is not so far removed from reality as to be a total misrepresentation.

The evident blessing of God on many new indepen-dent assemblies and networks puts charismatic renewal within the mainline Churches in a different perspective. It prevents all forms of complacency and self-congratulation about renewal in our own ranks. It reminds us how the full grace of renewal that the Lord desires to pour out is dependent on our Churches repenting for their disobedi-ence, and humbly acknowledging the depth of their need for renewal. It reminds us that all grace of renewal is the sheer mercy of God.

## The Challenge to the Non-Denominationals

A different challenge faces the non-denominationals. Their rapid growth, their initial freedom from restrictive patterns and structures, their youthful dynamism can all foster attitudes of spiritual superiority; they can think 'we are where it is all happening' and 'we are the Church of the future', with correspondingly dismissive attitudes towards the older Churches. To those tempted to think in this way, the Word of the Lord says:

> Do not boast over those branches. If you do, consider this: You do not support the root, but the root supports you. You will say then, 'Branches were broken off so that I could be grafted in.' Granted. But they were broken off because of unbelief, and you stand by faith. Do not be arrogant, but be afraid. For if God did not spare the natural branches, he will not spare you either. (Rom 11:18–21 NIV)

The new independent charismatic churches and networks represent a particular grace of God, which is a grace not only for them but for all. Being outside the historic structures is both a strength and a weakness. The strength is a greater freedom to express and develop, without compromise, the new life of Pentecost with its abundant gifts. Externally unrestrained by set traditions or the vested interests of venerable institutions, they are free to develop forms of worship and ministry as they desire and see fit. This can facilitate a greater openness to the promptings of the Holy Spirit, but it can also produce a greater vulnerability to less desirable patterns. The weakness is that they are less rooted in Christian history. Groups that are new and consciously rejecting the reigning traditions are always in danger of throwing out some gold with the dross. While they are not without historical antecedents, the exhilaration of 'the new wave' rarely fosters historical awareness. For those independent leaders conscious of belonging to a nonconformist heritage, the past is a potential source of important lessons rather than a heritage with which they are forced to grapple. Without liturgy, creeds or canonized saints, they do not inherit from the past the riches of doctrine, of worship, of spiritual wisdom that are the precious heritage of the ancient Churches of both East and West. They lack the organic structure and cohesion of the original tree, with the protection this gives against aberrant novelty and unconscious surrender to the spirit of the age.

Freedom from inherited embodiments of Christian life and ministry can have advantages, particularly in the short term, but it can be a liability, especially in the long run. For embodiments always contain more than present consciousness registers. This hidden surplus is the basis for all profounder penetration of God's gift, whether from the embodiment in God's Word or the embodiments in sacramental liturgy, forms of communal life or patterns of ministry.

If the grace of God through the non-denominationals is to bear its full fruit, they have to recognize their own indebtedness to those from whom many of them came out. They must recognize and thank God for every gift and grace they have been given. But to go beyond awareness of being in some way a sign of God's purpose to present themselves as the whole, as being simply the restored Church, is to exalt themselves beyond the call of God. They are a sign from the Lord, and are potentially a blessing to the wider Church; they are neither 'the scourge of the sects,' nor are they a replacement for the historic expressions of the Church any more than the Gentiles were a replacement for the Jews.

The independent churches have received from the Lord something vital enabling them to evangelize and plant new bodies of committed believers in a way and to a degree that the mainline Churches are not yet able to do. But for the proper nurture of this new life and its anchoring in structures that serve the people, they deeply need the riches and the wisdom that are passed on, often in forms that are hidden, perhaps even imprisoned, within the older Christian traditions. Much depends on the openness and the humility of the new churches.

If the new churches can accept their role of being both a sign and a vital catalyst, refusing the temptation to be simply the Church, then the way will be open for a deep mutual enrichment between the new and the old. The gifts of God in the new independent churches can spur the mainline Churches to repentance, stirring them perhaps to a holy envy, similar to Paul's hope in Romans 11:14. The humility of the older Churches can help the new assemblies to address their own weaknesses and to open themselves to the deep and constant witness of the Spirit mediated within the historic traditions. This openness can help them to avoid the dangers of narrow exclusiveness, of a confining literalism, of facile oppositions unknown to the biblical tradition. In particular, the older traditions bear witness to the constant struggle between spirit and flesh, between fidelity to the Lord and accommodation to the world. Their witness to the role of cross and resurrection in the experience of trial and suffering can protect the new churches from the great dangers of a 'gospel of success' which distorts and trivializes the great works of Jesus.

## Recognition, and then Theology

It is too soon for any agreement to be possible between all streams in the charismatic movement concerning the Spirit's work in the Church. What is possible, but only through the humbling grace of the Spirit, is for the old and the new to recognize the presence of the Spirit of life in the other, however great the difficulties of explaining this theologically. Christians in liturgical-sacramental traditions can recognize the presence of the Spirit in new assemblies and networks, as they already generally admit the Spirit's work in the older Free Church traditions. Christians in the new churches can recognize the presence of the Spirit in the older Churches they have been tempted to write off as dead and beyond resuscitation. Both can be led to see that these Spirit-filled

believers on the 'other side' are not simply such in spite
of their Churches and denominations, but are blessed and
enriched through their ministrations.

There remains of course an immense theological task,
of understanding the relationship between the Spirit's
work within the historic structures and the Spirit's work
outside them. This calls for expansion and deep renewal
in everyone's theology of the Church. Lest anyone think
there is something abnormal about having spiritual certainties with minimal theological elaboration, we must
see this as the condition of the primitive Church of the
first generations after Pentecost. In fact, the greater the
activity of the Spirit in any age, the more extensive will
be the theological catch-up needed.

## Non-Denominational Groups and Messianic Judaism

The non-denominational charismatic groupings began
to flourish about the same time as Messianic Judaism
appeared. It seems quite possible that there is a connection, for Messianic Judaism itself represents a form
of non-denominational Christianity. This fact also points
to another form of disobedience on the part of the older
Churches, particularly the Catholic and the Orthodox.
For the historic acceptance of the demise of Jewish
Christianity and the enforced repudiation of their Jewishness by Jewish converts to (Gentile) Christianity are contrary to the plan of God revealed especially in Ephesians
2:14–16 and 3:1–6. In this situation of an exclusively
Gentile Church, the only possible way for the rise of
Messianic synagogues celebrating Jewish feasts and
observances and confessing Jesus as Messiah is as
non-denominational congregations outside the historic
Churches.

In fact, Messianic Jewish groups have been developing
in a similar pattern to Gentile non-denominational groupings. Many congregations are being established, linked
through networks and associations of congregations, with
no over-all supervisory or co-ordinating agency.[2] So just

as there are different emphases from one network to another in the independent charismatic sector, there are differences between the Messianic Jewish groups (with varying attitudes to Zionism and the state of Israel).

Messianic Judaism can cast an important light on the non-denominational phenomenon. For the Jews have always recognized the right of Jewish believers, at least Jewish men, to form synagogues. While none could appoint himself as priest (Heb 5:4), they did have the right to form synagogues, without needing the approval of Jewish authority. Thus primitive Christianity inherited and made its own a polity combining apostolic mission (those sent and empowered by Jesus to lead the Church) and free association (the formation of Jewish Christian synagogues).

In this light, the problem of new divisions caused by the formation of new assemblies may arise from inherited Church patterns giving much less scope to this second element, the right to form synagogues. The newly-formulated right of association in the new Roman Catholic Code of Canon Law represents an official though limited step in the restoration of this concept.

We should then be open to the possibility that Messianic Judaism may hold the clue to the future of non-denominational charismatic Christianity. That is to say, the Messianic Jews link the oldest tradition with a radically new initiative. They challenge the older Churches as to whether a place for Messianic Jews can be provided in their communion. The working out of this challenge may show the way to acceptance of the independent churches and their networks, and prevent their becoming new denominations, a conclusion they energetically repudiate but others often regard as inevitable.

# Conclusion

Both the series of surprises of the Spirit in the successive extensions of the Pentecostal blessing, and the non-denominational explosion represent distinct but complementary works of the Holy Spirit. Both have a significant purpose in the plan of God. Each needs the other, both for its own humility and for its own authenticity.

The astonishing rise of independent charismatic churches is a chastening reminder to the mainline Churches of the insufficiency of their response to the profligacy of God's gift of the Spirit in this century. The charismatic renewal in the mainline Churches is a sign of God's enduring mercy and faithfulness to those who bear the name of Christ and to the Churches that have embodied the new covenant throughout the centuries. The outpouring of the Spirit among the Messianic Jews is a sign of God's unfailing love for the children of Abraham and of God's faithfulness to the promises of the old covenant. The non-denominational explosion does not negate the significance of the series of surprises of the Lord's work of gathering God's scattered children into one. It serves however to remind all that unity can only be on the basis of complete openness to the Spirit, and total obedience to the Word. It cautions all against any naive optimism and against all attempted short-cuts.

In fact, the complementarity of renewal in the mainline Churches and new moves outside their framework is rooted in who God is. Because God is God, God cannot be confined to any framework, even those that God has formed. God's actions outside the structures expose the arrogance of those who mistake stewardship over God's gifts for legal possession and control. But because God is God and not a mere creature, the historic embodiments of Christian life coming from God's hand can never lose that imprint, which has to be greater than sinful minds can fathom. Neither the greatest disobedience nor the foulest corruption can totally remove the handiwork of God, whether in the Church or in the creation around us. For the creature is not God. But in the Church, there is the deeper faithfulness of God to everything that bears the mark of God's Son.

# CHAPTER TWENTY-THREE

# ITS PLACE IN THE
# WIDER PICTURE

At the end of this study of the Pentecostal and charismatic movements, it is worth adding some reflections on their relationship to the wider Church and to other contemporary works of the Holy Spirit. Because the focus has been on a particular work of the Spirit, the impression could easily be given that this alone is of significance. Since major claims are being made for the Pentecostal–charismatic phenomenon (expressed in the 'Glory' of the title), though with important qualifications (indicated by 'Shame'), it is important to clarify what is being claimed, and what is not being claimed.

## What is Being Claimed

Clearly it is being argued that the Pentecostal and charismatic movements represent an event of major significance in the purposes of God. This is indicated by their relationship both to Pentecost and to the Parousia. It can also be seen from the extraordinary transconfessional character and scope of this grace. It is hardly possible to recognize that the grace of Pentecost is being poured out afresh on the Christian world, and then treat this phenomenon as just one among a number of interesting things that are happening.

Because of its sovereign character and its ecumenical range, this current of grace and life affects every aspect of Church life: prayer and worship, mission and evangelism, ministry and service, theology and hermeneutics, education, formation and spirituality. It cannot be reduced to a movement primarily concerned with only one or two of these essential tasks of the Church.

## What is not Being Claimed

As the first chapter has indicated, it is not being claimed that Pentecostal and charismatic believers are super-Christians, looking down on all lesser breeds with disdain or contempt. These movements have more than their share of scandals, and in their gracedness manifest a fragility that should foster humility and evoke fervent intercession.

Nor is it being claimed that the Holy Spirit is not at work in other Christian circles, nor even that the Spirit is not significantly at work elsewhere. God's love and mercy are so abundant that they overflow all human categories, much though our narrow minds may try to limit the Lord.

The Pentecostal and charismatic movements are not the only movements of the Holy Spirit because (a) they are not the Church, but a gift of God for the Church[1]; and (b) there are many other movements and currents of the Spirit in the Christian world. For these reasons, no work or movement of the Holy Spirit can be self-contained or self-sufficient.

## Other Movements of the Spirit

Despite, or maybe because of, the widespread apostasy or leakage from Christian faith in many countries thought of as Christian nations, the twentieth century has seen a remarkable number of movements of spiritual revival and renewal throughout the Christian world. It is not the purpose here to provide a catalogue of such movements and currents, much less to assess them. It will suffice to mention a few of the more outstanding examples; for only the most prejudiced person could maintain that these instances do not manifest the presence and power of the Holy Spirit.

From the Protestant Evangelical world, the ministry of Billy Graham has had an indubitable impact, and its spiritual fruit has been widely recognized. The work of Campus Crusade for Christ with their practical emphasis on the four spiritual laws has had important results, including some collaboration with the Catholic Church. In the Reformed world, two communities have had a major impact in very differing ways: the Iona Community in Scotland, and the Taizé Community in France. In the Catholic Church, the spiritual movements known as Focolari (founded by Chiara Lubich from Italy) and Cursillo (founded by Bishop Hervas from Majorca, Spain) have impressed all who know their work. Both groupings have had significant impact beyond the Roman Catholic Church.

The movements and fellowships cited are not all the same kind of entity; they are neither all of equal significance nor have they all had the same range of influence. All that is being said is that they are all evident works of the Holy Spirit in this century. Their visible impact is attested by their influences extending far beyond the Churches and milieux of their origins.

## The Distinctive Charismatic Contribution

The recognition of the Pentecostal and charismatic movements as 'gifts' to the wider Church requires greater precision in identifying the heart of the gift. This study suggests that their particular contribution is to be found in the sovereign character of the Lord's action in them and through them. The directness of relationship to the Lord and the Spirit, and the immediacy of communication opened up are intrinsic and central to this grace. They ground the appropriateness of the term 'baptized in the Holy Spirit'. In this light, the spiritual gifts can be seen as the distinctive symbols of this sovereign activity of God and of this immediacy of 'vertical' relationship.

This interpretation is to locate the distinctiveness of the Pentecostal–charismatic outpouring at what we may call a *transcendental* level. Their basic contribution is not to be found in particulars (liturgy, doctrinal emphases, prayer techniques, evangelistic strategies, or even the

gifts), but in the very way in which God is acting and
communicating. Because the distinctiveness lies at this
transcendental level, it has the potential to affect all
particulars.

The hiddenness of God's self-revelation in Christ influences the directness of God's self-communication and
action through the Spirit of Pentecost. Being baptized
in the Spirit does not exempt the Christian from the
limitations of the age of the Church. But it does involve
a vivid knowledge of the Lord, that is itself a pledge and
hope for the perfect vision to come. 'Beloved, we *are* God's
children *now*; it does not yet appear what we shall be, but
we know that when he appears we shall be like him, for
we shall see him as he is' (1 John 3:2; italics mine).

While locating distinctiveness at this higher level is
making a bigger claim, it is making lesser claims concerning the particulars. This is ultimately why there is
nothing inherently incompatible between being baptized
in the Spirit and belonging to or being influenced by any
of these other movements or currents of the Spirit.

## Relationship with the Wider Church

If the distinctive contribution of the Pentecostal and
charismatic movements lies at this transcendental level,
then we have to ask how this grace of baptism in the Spirit
relates to all the structures of the Church and the forms of
mediation in Word and sacrament that have been passed
down through the centuries.

One explanation that has to be ruled out is to argue that
the immediacy of charismatic faith should be inserted
alongside the mediated patterns of received Church life.
This would be to accept a devaluation of Word and
sacrament by denying the immediacy of God's presence
in and through them.

The only satisfactory understanding of their relationship is to see that the Pentecostal–charismatic experience
involves a rediscovery of the nature of all God's dealings
with believers in Christ. That is to say, the Christian baptized in the Spirit is able, through a particular experience

of the immediacy of the Lord, to rediscover the immediacy and directness of the Lord's presence and activity in every aspect of Christian life, especially in Word and sacrament. The difference between charismatic patterns of Christian experience and ministry and others is not that the former have an immediacy to the Lord and the latter do not; it is that the immediacy and directness of the Lord in the latter are less manifest. Charismatic experience of the Lord thus invites Christians to rediscover the true *mediation* in Word and sacrament, that is to experience *the Lord* in and through them, in place of any *substitutive* role whereby these instruments in effect replace rather than mediate the Lord.

This may throw light on the reasons in God's providence why this grace was first bestowed 'outside the gates'. One of the deepest problems in the mainline Churches is that the structures of mediation have assumed such a dominance that they can obscure the immediacy and directness of God. The structures of mediation are absolutely necessary and in their root are divinely-given and mandated. But in this situation of occlusion of the immediate, it may be that only a grace of immediacy outside the structures could be an effective instrument of restoring the immediacy of the Lord in Word and sacrament. In the origins, the immediate preceded the mediated, the charismatic preceded the institutional; for the latter draw all their meaning from the former.[2]

## Relationship with Other Currents

Historically, some other movements can be seen to have played a preparatory role in opening people to the modern grace of 'Pentecost'. It is evident that various currents of blessing in the Wesleyan and Holiness movements prepared the way for the Pentecostal revival. With the charismatic movement, evident preparatory roles were played among Catholics in the United States by the Cursillo movement and to a lesser extent Marriage Encounter, and in Poland by the Light and Life movement (formerly Oasis). It was true of the Order of St Luke and of Camps Farthest Out among many mainline Protestants.

However, it would be wrong for Pentecostals and charismatics to draw the conclusion that the only purpose of these other movements was to prepare for baptism in the Spirit. Every work of the Spirit is fundamentally for God and for Christ. To reduce any movement or grace to the level of means, even the means to a higher or deeper grace, is to reduce the Holy Spirit to an instrument.

Thus, the first principle for the interaction of different movements of the Spirit in the Church is mutual recognition and respect in Christian *koinonia*. What is to be respected is the specific work of the Holy Spirit. Each work of the Holy Spirit is necessarily complementary to all other works of the Holy Spirit, even if we cannot understand how they fit together. They cannot be rightfully opposed, any more than one charism can be opposed to another. As Paul says of the spiritual gifts in 1 Corinthians 12: 'All these are inspired by one and the same Spirit, who apportions to each one individually as he wills' (12:11).

Notwithstanding the variety in the Spirit's creativity within the Churches, the fundamental work of the Spirit of God remains the same: the Holy Spirit always convicts of sin, and the Holy Spirit always glorifies Jesus Christ. No group or movement within the Church can claim a monopoly of these foundational works of the Holy Spirit. The profundity and significance of particular works of the Spirit will always be in direct proportion to the intensity of these two primordial activities of the Holy Spirit.

If the distinctive contribution of the Pentecostal and charismatic movements lies at the transcendental level of God's immediate mode of self-communication, then it ought to manifest most clearly the conviction of sin and the manifestation of Jesus. Where this is not the case, the core-gift of these movements has not been grasped, and they are being corrupted into something far less wonderful. This dreadful possibility leads us into the next chapter.

# CHAPTER TWENTY-FOUR

# ADDRESSING THE SHAME

The title of this book expresses the mixed character of the Pentecostal and charismatic movements. They manifest the glory of the Lord and his gifts, but they also provide cause for shame in the ways Pentecostal and charismatic Christians have abused these gifts. Most chapters have focused on the glory, on the work of the Holy Spirit in this outpouring of divine life and power. This focus is not a reversion to triumphalism after a token recognition of human frailty. Rather, the importance of these movements lies in the divine gift, not in the deviations. Grasping their significance in God's purpose requires an identification of what is most surely of the Holy Spirit. This is the necessary starting-point for serious theological reflection.

However, the ambiguities, the weaknesses and the manifestations of sin cannot simply be ignored. They have to be faced, not only for the sake of accuracy and fairness, not just for the sake of humility, but because the sin in these movements undermines their spiritual power and frustrates the purpose for which God has sent them. Identifying the ambiguities, the weaknesses and the sin is important so that all may be clear on what has to be opposed and resisted, if these currents of grace are to realize their God-given purpose.

## Are We Naive?

Should we be surprised at the shameful elements in Pentecostal–charismatic revival–renewal or even at their extent? Should we be surprised at the moral humiliation of famed preachers or at financial irregularities in major ministries? Should we be astonished at the break-up of charismatic communities previously admired as models? Or at the rivalries between charismatic celebrities? Does it amaze us to discover that big figures sometimes have big egos?

Though these things will sadden all those who truly love the Lord Jesus, none should surprise us – at least if we have some idea of what Jesus knew: 'for he himself knew what was in man' (John 2:25). There are three main reasons why we should not be surprised: (a) the condition of fallen human nature; (b) the particular weaknesses of modern Western society; and (c) Satan's hatred for the work of God.

## The Roots of Our Weakness

### The Condition of Fallen Human Nature

We are all children of Adam and Eve. We belong to a tarnished line of which Scripture says 'there is no distinction; since all have sinned and fall short of the glory of God' (Rom 3:22–23). We have an ache for eternity and a bias towards self. The classics of Christian literature show how the saints of every age have known the absolute necessity of combatting and not giving ground to this bias of fallen human nature.

Those who experience the exhilaration of baptism in the Spirit are often vulnerable to a naive optimism that discounts the possibility of moral lapse. The euphoria of Pentecostal–charismatic experience can lead people to think that they are no longer subject to the downward pull of the flesh. Jesus has made victory possible through his blood and cross, but he has not yet granted us exemption from this fallen condition.

Those who have experienced a new degree of immediacy in relationship to the divine are always in danger of forgetting or neglecting the limitations that belong to the age of the Church between the two comings of Jesus.

Thus charismatic and Pentecostal Christians can speak as though all is now unveiled, as though the divine is in no way hidden, as though Christians do not have to follow their master on the way of humiliation and of suffering. All baptized in the Spirit have the responsibility to affirm all that God has truly done; they must bear witness to the elements of real immediacy, the real opening of the heavenlies, the real access to the divine throne. But they must do so in a way that also recognizes that they are still 'earthen vessels' (2 Cor 4:7), that they still only 'know in part' (1 Cor 13:12), and that their 'life is hid with Christ in God' (Col 3:3).

## The Particular Weaknesses of Modern Western Society

We live in a culture oriented towards self: presenting self-aggrandizement as worldly wisdom, self-gratification as a human right, and self-fulfilment as the all-encompassing ideal. The world around urges us to pursue comfort, fun and achievement. The unpleasant is kept at a distance, at least for the more privileged; pain is anaesthetized, and death hidden from view or, where unavoidable, sanitized and dehumanized. Success depends on cut-throat competition. Instant acquisition is lauded, the long haul disdained.

This cameo may seem harsh. But who can deny that this is the picture dangled before millions each day as they feast their eyes on the television screen? Who can deny the seductive power of this mirage? Even those alarmed by this crass materialism find it hard to remain uncontaminated. Perceptive Eastern Europeans have remarked that the attitudes induced by two generations of atheistic Communism will take many years to get out of their systems, not only from its supporters but also from its most courageous opponents. In the West we have years of indoctrination and conditioning in the consumer society, in the 'feel-good' world of the supermarket and instant entertainment. These are immediately threatened but not instantly removed by a sudden influx of the Holy Spirit.

It should not surprise us that this wonderful grace of God in the Pentecostal and charismatic movements can be subverted and corrupted by our self-oriented culture. It is not hard to see how God's gifts can be turned into tools to serve our ego-fulfilment; how the newly-discovered power of God can be harnessed to advance our prosperity, our careers, our families; how people consumed by ambition for success in the world can become consumed by ambition for success in ministry – and still believe that they are zealous ministers of the Lord.

## Satan's Hatred for the Work of God

A third factor in the genesis of the shameful is the role of Satan and of evil spirits. The experience of holy people throughout the ages has always been that the opposition and malice of Satan become apparent precisely when God is being taken seriously and the Holy Spirit is clearly at work. The pattern is shown in the life of Jesus who is tempted by the devil in the wilderness immediately after being filled with the Spirit at his baptism.

Scripture suggests that Satan is aware that his days are numbered, and that his efforts to destroy the Church will become more frenzied as the second coming approaches (see Rev 12:12). If it is true that this Pentecostal–charismatic outpouring of the Spirit heralds the return of the Lord, it is not surprising that it attracts the most vicious attacks of the Evil One.

Recognition of the opposition of Satan is not a denial of the responsibility of Pentecostal and charismatic Christians for their sins and scandalous behaviour. What it does mean is that a global work of God on the scale of the Pentecostal and charismatic movements has to be a prime target for the forces of darkness.

Any welcome given to Pentecostal–charismatic revival–renewal that does not recognize these negative influences subverting the work of the Spirit is naive. Because leaders are implicated in what is shameful, it is evident that leaders too can share this naïveté.

# The Shameful Subverts the Divine Majesty and Fulness

The subversion of God's grace does not usually begin with outright malice and hypocrisy. It happens through the subversion of those who at the outset had an authentic encounter with the Lord. They may well at that time have experienced a dramatic conversion and transformation in their lives.

Subversion of the work of the Spirit occurs through subordination of the spirit to human powers of mind and will, instead of submission of these powers of the human soul to the Spirit. When people are baptized in the Spirit and are awakened to the spiritual realm, learned patterns of self-promotion, self-aggrandizement and self-defence do not instantly disappear. This is when a new conflict breaks out between the new life of the Spirit (*pneuma*) and the old patterns that Paul calls flesh (*sarx*).

Because the Spirit of God is more powerful than, and totally opposed to, all sin and self-will, the initial impulses after authentic reception of the Spirit are towards the kingdom of God. It is when the underlying drives are not recognized and not reckoned as crucified with Christ that the generally slow, but certainly undermining, process occurs. For the undealt-with flesh will always subvert the life of the Spirit (see Gal 4:29; 5:17).

In an environment of wise leadership and solid biblical teaching, the new Christian will be helped to recognize elements that are fleshly (*sarkikos*) or soulish (*psychikos*). As the convert experiences the truth enacted at baptism, that the old nature was crucified with Christ on the cross, the zeal for Christian service will flow more and more from the new heart that is the spirit. From being *psychikos*, the Christian becomes *pneumatikos*, that is spiritual (see 1 Cor 2:14–15).

The problems arise with Christians who are unwilling to submit themselves to wise leadership and sound teaching. This danger is much greater in Pentecostal–charismatic circles, precisely because being baptized in

the Spirit is such a joyous experience, and because it
opens people up to hear the Lord in their spirits. In a
situation that requires greater wisdom and more discernment, immature charismatic Christians can think that
these gifts are less necessary – because it is so evident
from inner feelings and outward results that they have
the Spirit, that God speaks to them, that their ministry
produces results.

## The Danger of Subjectivism

The forms of subversion so far mentioned have concen-
trated on the failings of the fleshly and self-centred, that
is from lack of effective sanctification in the believer.
Often linked to these in practice, but distinct in their
effects, are the dangers that stem from subjective imbal-
ances in faith and in doctrine.

Precisely because the Pentecostal and charismatic
movements have opened up Christians to the experience
of hearing God's voice and to receiving interior revelation
of the Word of God, these movements run the risks of
an unbalanced subjectivism. This can take the form of
doctrinal aberrations apparently sanctioned by personal
experience, but not confirmed by the Word of God or by
the apostolic faith. It can also take the form of imbalance:
that of concentration on the content of such messages or
communications and insufficient attention to the rest of
divine revelation.

One particular danger may be mentioned here. It is
the combination among some Catholics of a charismatic
emphasis on contemporary revelation and a Marian devotion of a strongly apocalyptic character. In some places,
this combination has almost taken over and displaced
Catholic charismatic renewal. Its fruits appear to be
highly questionable. It seems to have happened to Catholics touched in some way by God through the charismatic
renewal, but who have a very weak knowledge of the
gospel. Instead of their renewal experience opening them
to the saving work of Jesus on the cross and the power
of the Holy Spirit to transform, they have majored on

revelations and messages. Bringing this fascination into a context of traditional Catholic Marian piety has often been disastrous both for charismatic renewal, in which all inner revelation needs to be submitted to the objective faith-revelation 'once for all delivered to the saints' (Jude 3), and for the older forms of Marian piety, which were not focused on constant messages but, in their better expressions, on penitence for sin and the call to holiness.

## Protection against Subversion

To protect God's sovereign grace against subversion, we must look first to the Lord. The Lord who gives this life knows how to protect it and cause it to grow. 'I planted, Apollos watered, but God gave the growth' (1 Cor 3:6). Churches and fellowships that cultivate and reverence the following elements will surely experience the protection of the Lord:

### (1)  Honouring the entire Word of God

Since subversion of God's grace often occurs through particular truths or emphases being made the centre and test of everything, a powerful protection lies in a conscious effort to take seriously the fulness of divine revelation and the total witness of Scripture. All doctrinal reductionism involves a submission of the mystery of Christ to a merely human logic that eliminates its infinite ineffability in favour of easily grasped simplicities.

The more we open ourselves to the Holy Spirit, the more we are confronted by the majesty of the living God: the God before whom nothing impure can stand, the God who rebukes Job for his ignorant words (Job 38:2), the God whose voice breaks the cedars (Ps 29:5), the God at whose word believers tremble (Isa 66:2), the God who is a consuming fire (Heb 12:29). Similarly, the Spirit reveals the real Jesus, who is most fully man but also he who 'reflects the glory of God and bears the very stamp of his nature, upholding the universe by his word of power' (Heb 1:3). The Christian filled with the Spirit

is ever growing in the knowledge and love of God and of
Jesus Christ.

## (2)  All the Means of Salvation

God has equipped the Church with all the ministries and
powers necessary to effect God's purpose. 'Put on the
whole armour of God, that you may be able to stand
against the wiles of the devil' (Eph 6:11). The following
verses mention truth, righteousness, the gospel of peace,
faith, the Word of God, prayer in the Spirit (6:14–18). To
these items of spiritual armour, we should add as means
of divine life the sacraments, in which the church community enacts the Word of life, especially the dominical
sacraments of baptism and eucharist. We should know
and call upon the power in the blood and the cross of
Jesus, and in his holy name. We cannot afford not to
utilize any equipment, any means of deliverance and
sanctification, that the Lord has given to the Church.

## (3)  Fellowship in the Body of Christ

The Holy Spirit always builds the *koinonia* of the body
of Christ. Christians growing in the Spirit should be
experiencing deeper and wider fellowship with fellow-
believers. Such fellowship can be a valuable protection
against imbalance and oddity. It can put individual leaders and assemblies in touch with the tradition of orthodox
Christian faith in theology, christology, soteriology and
eschatology. It can be a modern application of the dictum
of Vincent of Lerins (fifth century) who distinguished
orthodoxy from heresy by the test: *Quod ubique, quod
semper, quod ab omnibus*, that is, that which is orthodox
has been held by everyone everywhere and at all times.
The fulness of Christian faith cannot be known in isolation, but results from a fulness of fellowship.

## (4)  Respect for Due Authority

All Christians, but especially Christians who appeal to
the guidance of the Spirit, need to respect the authority

that the Lord has placed in the Church. There are significant differences here between different Christian traditions, ranging from Catholic insistence on the papal ministry to those Christians who emphasize the autonomy of the local congregation. Lack of accountability to any Church authority is a dangerous condition.

> Remember your leaders, those who spoke to you the word of God; consider the outcome of their life, and imitate their faith . . . Obey your leaders and submit to them; for they are keeping watch over your souls, as men who will have to give account. Let them do this joyfully, and not sadly, for that would be of no advantage to you. (Heb 13:7, 17)

All our ideas, our projects, our impulses need to be tested. 'Test everything' (1 Thess 5:21). No one is the best judge in their own case. The instinct to react, rebel and denounce at the first sign of opposition to our ideas comes from the spirit of the world, not the Spirit of Jesus. Christians who have a living relationship with the Lord will be tenacious in their faith but will also know their capacity to be wrong. They will value properly constituted authority as a service from the Lord, not as opposition to be swept aside.

## (5)  A Willingness to Suffer

Not only will the power of the Spirit arouse the opposition of the world (in the Johannine sense) and the hatred of Satan, it may increase conflict within the Christian community. Christians baptized in the Spirit have to be willing to suffer for their witness. Fidelity to the Lord does not mean hiding our light beneath a bushel. We are called to follow the example of Jesus himself, who suffered at the hands of the legitimate authorities of the Jewish people, and thereby gained the salvation of all, Jew and Gentile. The willingness to suffer for one's convictions, and to do so in humility and without counter-accusation – this is the way placed before us in Scripture as the way of the prophets and of the Lord himself.

Those truly taught of the Spirit have a prophetic witness to give in the midst of God's people. They owe it to God not to dilute the prophetic word out of fear of rejection, owe it to his people to speak it in love, and owe it to themselves to do so, humbly acknowledging their own unworthiness and their own need to be taught. The demeanour of the Christian witness in the face of opposition is often the surest sign of the Spirit that inspired the message.

# CHAPTER TWENTY-FIVE

# WHERE DO WE GO FROM HERE?

If Christians baptized in the Spirit are to hold this work of God together, despite the doctrinal differences that need to be resolved, they need a common vision. Such a vision would serve as a framework to deepen unity and prevent further division. The principles developed in this book are offered as potential contributions to a framework within which all streams within the Pentecostal and charismatic movements could work and collaborate. The fundamental elements in such a vision would include:

(1) The Pentecostal–charismatic outpouring of the Spirit in this century bears the hallmarks of a sovereign work of God for the renewal of Christian life in all its dimensions and the reconciliation of separated Christian traditions and Churches.

(2) The central grace of this outpouring is the Lord Jesus baptizing in the Holy Spirit. This is first of all a corporate work as on the Day of Pentecost, which both forms and enlivens the body of Christ. It restores the level of life and the immediacy to the Trinity that belong by divine gift to the people of the new covenant.

(3) This grace is both ecumenical and eschatological. It is poured out on all God's covenanted people, in all Christian traditions, old and new, and on the people of the old covenant. It is essentially oriented towards the preparation of God's people as one renewed and restored Church for the return of Jesus, whether imminent or not in terms of human chronology.

(4) The way of renewal and reconciliation always

involves a summons to repentance for our sins and the sins of our fathers.

(5)  The different streams (Pentecostal, Protestant charismatic, Catholic charismatic, Messianic Jewish and independent charismatic) all belong to the one over-all outpouring of the Spirit.

## The Responsibility of Each Church

Each Church grouping has a responsibility before God for its own faithfulness to the Word of life. Each body or network of believers has a responsibility to preserve at all costs and to live as deeply as possible all that the Spirit of God has given. Each Church body has a responsibility to repent for its infidelity to the Lord. This means seriously seeking the sifting of the Spirit of God to make clear what in its inheritance is of the Spirit, and therefore to be treasured with tenacity, and what is a defilement for which to repent.

There are major differences between different types of Church body. There are at least three main categories: (a) the ancient Churches of East and West (Roman Catholic, Eastern Orthodox, and Oriental Orthodox); (b) the Churches of the Reformation that split off from the ancient Churches, often in national blocs; and (c) the Free Churches, formed on a principle of voluntary association.[1] What the Spirit confirms as gold, and what the Spirit convicts as dross, will follow different patterns from category to category.

For the Roman Catholic Church, the structures of universal communion in baptism and eucharist, in the threefold ministry of bishop, priest and deacon, and the primatial ministry of the pope as successor to Peter are part of the gold, gifts of the Spirit of God essential to the constitution of the Church in this world. But that does not mean that the ways these elements have developed in history, the forms in which they have been clothed, the arguments with which they have been defended, are all equally the work of the Spirit of God. Ecumenically, the way ahead for the Roman Catholic Church is to welcome the sifting Spirit: to want the light of the Spirit to illumine the Spirit's gift in these churchly elements; to want the light of the Spirit to convict of all that is an impediment to the Lord. It is impossible to have instant discernment without prolonged prayer and searching of heart. We should resist the temptation to claim immediate total vision, as though all that is of God and all that is not can be instantly identified and separated, whether by the most ardent defenders of the tradition or by its sharpest critics.

With the more recent traditions of the voluntary type, there is a less encumbered inheritance, indeed there may be ideological resistance to the very idea of tradition. Whereas the Spirit will convict the ancient Churches of defilement in the many elements coming down from the past, the Spirit is likely to convict the younger Churches of over-hasty rejection of elements dismissed as 'dead tradition' and 'mere human works'. Here the Spirit prises open the closed mind, undermining the certainties that come from human stubbornness rather than divine faith. Here too time is needed for deep heart-searching before the Lord, but in contrast to the ancient traditions, it may focus more on what has been rejected than what is affirmed.

How can such disparate bodies possibly come together? That is not our immediate responsibility. Our immediate task is to allow, indeed to want, the Holy Spirit's sifting of our Church inheritance, and to plead for it before the throne of God. Trying to bring the Churches together when this sifting has not occurred, or it has not really penetrated the life and thinking of the people, is an enterprise inviting frustration and disappointment.

Begging the Holy Spirit to illuminate and convict is the only way of avoiding the dilemma of rigid conservatism or unbridled reform.[2] Christians, who are equally open to the Spirit's work of revealing Jesus, and the conviction of sin, will be determined to preserve the witness of the Spirit and not to allow anything not of the Spirit to impede God's work.

# The Heart of Each Tradition

Constant seeking of the light of the Holy Spirit on the
Word of God, and on the teaching and life of our Churches
will lead to illumination and purification. Not only will
the Spirit illuminate and confirm the divine work in each
tradition, but the Spirit will reveal, not a disconnected list
of truths, but an organic whole with a heart and a core.

The heart of each tradition is that to which believers
cling most tenaciously. This is that for which people
have been willing to die. While it is possible to adhere
stubbornly to something with a demonic power, only
divinely revealed truths can be held with the God-given
certainty of faith. When we encounter other Christians
clinging tenaciously to teachings or practices for which
they are willing to suffer, we should presume that something God-given and precious lies at the heart of this
commitment. This applies equally to Catholic belief in
the papacy, to Orthodox convictions about conciliarity,
to Lutheran insistence on justification by faith, and to
Baptist adherence to the priesthood of all believers.

Since all authentic Christianity centres on Jesus Christ,
the heart of each Christian tradition is in some way
a facet of Jesus. Christians cling tenaciously to that
which they know, however inchoately or intuitively, was
given them by the Lord. Yes, this gift needs sifting from
associated ideas that come from human embellishment;
yes, it needs complementing by other gifts and cannot
stand on its own. But it is still a treasure, and those who
know it are right to cling to it. Each one's obligation is to
live such truths in as full and pure a way as possible, so
that their authenticity can be recognized by all.

## Mutual Solidarity

While each Church is primarily responsible to the Lord
for its own life and inheritance, it is not possible to
disavow responsibility for each other. This is part of
bearing each other's burdens (Gal 6:2).

The mutual responsibility of Church traditions for each
other at least involves the following elements:

(1) *Celebrating in common what all have received from the Spirit.* Because the work of the Spirit of its nature impels to unity, we have an obligation to celebrate in thanksgiving before God that which now unites us in Christ. This worship should acknowledge the shared gift as a first-fruit of the full promise in which together we hope.

(2) *Sharing when the Spirit convicts our Churches of sin.* Because our sins divide us from one another, conviction of our sins and the sins of our fathers necessarily affects our relations with other Christian Churches. We should then as Churches ask forgiveness from other Churches for the bad witness we have given.

(3) *With the responsibility to share goes the need to allow others to share with us.* When they ask forgiveness of their sins and those of their fathers, we must ask for the grace of the Spirit to forgive them. Both should ask what new possibilities of faith sharing are opened up by this mutual repentance.

(4) *Accepting and loving the work of the Holy Spirit wherever we find it.* Even if we cannot see immediately how a particular work of the Holy Spirit in another tradition could fit into or correlate with the life and teaching of our own Church, we should still thank God for it and affirm it in the others.

## The Holy Spirit Cannot But Build the Body of Christ

A nagging anxiety among many Christians in the mainline Churches needs to be addressed. It is not merely how such disparate groups of Christians can be brought together. It concerns the very possibility of bodies formed by free association ever becoming what Catholics and Orthodox would regard as Church. For Christians in these ancient traditions, the Church is first a historical reality to which they belong, and only secondarily a doctrine or a theory; the Church is constituted historically by the living Son of God, is given particular structures which humans are not free to dismiss, and

exists with an essential historical continuity. How can
Christians with such convictions recognize any corporate
churchly significance in bodies formed freely by human
association?

The Holy Spirit is truly the Spirit of God who cannot
but reveal and make present the person of Jesus, who
cannot but form the fellowship of the body of Christ,
who cannot but prepare for the return of the Lord. That
is to say, whenever human beings open up to the work
of God's Spirit, they are necessarily being led towards
Jesus, towards the communion of Jesus' Church, and
towards the final glorious kingdom. Whenever a person
confesses Jesus Christ as Lord and Saviour come in the
flesh, the Holy Spirit is at work. Whatever the deficiencies
of their understanding and exegesis, the grace at work in
them has an intrinsic impulse towards visible expression
in proclaimed Word and celebrated sacrament, an inner
direction towards the full reality of Church.

Because the Holy Spirit is the Spirit of God and the
Spirit of Christ, the presence of the Spirit always draws
and invites towards fulness in the divine Trinity. This
is a comforting thought for all Christians, because all
of our Churches are existentially deficient in some way,
whether in doctrine, structure or spiritual vitality, or a
combination of the above. From God's side, any sovereign
outpouring of the Holy Spirit cannot contradict what is
of the Spirit in the history of God's covenant people. It
must contain in seminal form that which is needed to
bring all God's covenant gifts to fruition. Unity requires
unreserved obedience to the Spirit outpoured, and an
openness to the full scope of what this gift already
contains.

## Have No Fear

When we look at this vast work of the Spirit in our day,
and when we acknowledge the many human weaknesses
and scandals that disfigure it, we must not be fearful,
whether participants or not. In the affairs of the Spirit,
we must develop confidence in the Spirit.

Fear – not to be confused with awe or reverence – is an enemy to God's work. Many believers can be beset by fear when they are faced with such a phenomenon:

- mainline Church leaders afraid of their people leaving their Church to join Pentecostal and independent assemblies then denounced as 'sects';
- ordained ministers afraid to trust the working of the Holy Spirit among the 'non-ordained';
- Church leaders afraid of a grass-roots ecumenism that cannot be controlled;
- Church leaders afraid of the effects of confessing mistakes in the history of their Church;
- leaders of new assemblies fearful of tradition and ancient structures;
- fear of impeding Christian–Jewish dialogue through any recognition of Messianic Judaism.

There is need for discernment. There is need for instruction. There is need for pastoral care. But fear will distort these essential functions. God is all-powerful, and when God Almighty pours out the Holy Spirit, God is powerful enough and loves enough to take care of his work. This is no recipe for rashness or a happy-go-lucky insouciance; no, what is needed is trust not fear: a trust that seeks the Lord's protection, a trust that seeks the Lord's wisdom, a trust that believes that the Lord is in charge and knows what the Spirit is doing, a trust that loves the Lord's work and all the people to whom it has come. We need the Spirit that led Paul to write: 'Do not quench the Spirit, do not despise prophesying, but test everything; hold fast what is good' (1 Thess 5:19–21).

# NOTES

## Introduction

1 Paternoster Press, Exeter, and The Word Among Us Press, Gaithersburg, Md., 1987.

## Chapter One

1 *Glimpses of Glory: Thirty Years of Community: the Story of Reba Place Fellowship* (Elgin, Illinois, Brethren Press, 1987).
2 Edward England (ed) *David Watson: A Portrait by His Friends* (Crowborough, Highland Books, 1985) p.212.
3 Quoted from article on 'Statistics, Global' in *Dictionary of Pentecostal and Charismatic Movements*, ed. Stanley M. Burgess and Gary B. McGee (Grand Rapids, Michigan, Zondervan, 1988).

## Chapter Two

1 A further surprise may yet be possible. In the last year, there have been reports on groups of Islamic converts to Christ among Turkish-language Muslims in Bulgaria. This revival, which does not appear to be the result of Christian evangelism and is said to be spreading quite rapidly, has led to the formation of 'Jesus-mosques'. For reasons similar to the Messianic Jews, these Bulgarian converts call themselves 'Messianic believers' rather than Christians. This development is still too new and insufficiently documented for it to be treated here among the series of evident surprises of the Holy Spirit in the twentieth century.

## Chapter Three

1 The 'Cretans and Arabians' (Acts 2:11) are evidently proselytes.

## Chapter Four

1 This was not an issue for the Roman Catholic Church, as the lack of ecumenical relations meant that Pentecostalism

appeared to Catholics, if they even knew of it, as a strictly Protestant issue.

2   Harald Bredesen was in fact baptized in the Spirit in 1946.

# Chapter Five

1   The article is omitted here as it is not present in the Greek text.

2   See, for example, the warning to 'flee from the wrath to come' (Matt 3:7).

3   This theophanic element in the 'Spirit-baptism' passages contrasts with 1 Cor 12:13, where Paul is referring to baptism in water, and insisting on the instrumentality of the Holy Spirit in forming believers into one body. This reading is confirmed by the baptismal references in 1 Cor 1:13–17 reproaching the Corinthians for their divisions.

# Chapter Six

1   E.g. Donald Dayton, *Theological Roots of Pentecostalism* (Metuchen, N.J., Scarecrow Press, 1987); Roland Wessels, 'The Spirit Baptism, Nineteenth Century Roots', *Pneuma* 14/2 (1992) pp. 127-157.

2   Also important was the expectation widely aroused by news of the Welsh revival that began in 1904.

3   A London Declaration (November 1909), 'The Baptism in the Holy Ghost' printed in *Confidence* (December 1909) pp. 287–288. The signatories were the earliest Pentecostal leaders and teachers in Britain; both those who later joined Pentecostal denominations, and Anglicans, Rev. Alexander Boddy and Mr. Cecil Polhill, who always remained in the Church of England.

4   The listing of the gifts is in the part omitted from the quotation.

5   *Victory*, (April 1909), p. 1.

6   Gordon Lindsey (ed.) *The New John G. Lake Sermons* (Dallas, Christ for the Nations Inc., no date), p. 14.

7   *The Acts of the Holy Spirit among the Episcopalians Today* (Los Angeles, Full Gospel Business Men, 1973) p. 28.

8   The imposition of hands to be baptized in the Holy Spirit had developed among some Pentecostals in the Latter Rain movement that began in Saskatchewan, Canada in the late 1940s.

9   *Theological and Pastoral Orientations on the Catholic Charismatic Renewal* (Ann Arbor, Word of Life, 1974) pp. 7–11.

# Chapter Seven

1   The early Pentecostal preacher, D. Wesley Myland, used Deut 11:10–21 for his basic teaching on the Latter Rain, and illustrated it further from Jer 3:2–5; Isa 30:15–26; Zech 10:1; Ps 65:9–13;

Job 29:23; Prov 16:15 and Ps 68:9–10 (*The Latter Rain Covenant*, Chicago, 1910. Chs. 1 & 2).

2   Oxford University Press, Oxford & New York, 1979.

3   *When God Calls* (London, Marshall, Morgan & Scott, 1970) p. 144.

4   Ann Arbor, Michigan, Servant Books, 1983.

5   Since 1991 renamed the Community of the Beatitudes.

6   Edward Irving, *Collected Writings*, Vol. V (London, Alexander Strahan, 1865) p. 500.

7   Ibid., p. 480.

8   As, for example, the Mary Sisters of Darmstadt, Germany, and the Community of the Beatitudes (formerly Lion of Juda) in France, cited above.

# Chapter Eight

1   See Chapter Nine.

2   This question is taken up in later chapters.

# Chapter Nine

1   See Chapter Twenty-two.

2   Another network of a closer kind is the Fellowship of Covenant. Ministries and conferences, associated with the leadership of Charles Simpson and centred in Mobile, Alabama.

3   The prosperity message of some American televangelists continues to be a source of controversy. Some studies have drawn attention to a deviant Christology in some prominent prosperity teachers.

4   My impression is that this pattern is more noticeable in the United States than in Great Britain.

5   The distinction between independent charismatics and independent Pentecostals is not always so clear in many of the Third World countries, where significant Pentecostal growth is much more recent.

6   The distinction between independent charismatics and independent Pentecostals is not always so clear in many of the Third World countries, where significant Pentecostal growth is much more recent.

# Chapter Eleven

1   *D'Aplomb sur la Parole de Dieu* (Valence, 1932) p. 13.

2   Ibid., p. 14.

3   Ibid., p. 39.

4   Translations from *D'Aplomb sur la Parole de Dieu* and from the charter are by the author.

## Chapter Twelve

1   See Jer 8:11, 22; 10:19; 14:17; 15:18.

## Chapter Seventeen

1   Full text in *One in Christ* 2/2 (1966) pp. 167–169.

## Chapter Eighteen

1   The word *apobolé* in Rom 11:15, often translated as 'rejection',
    is better rendered 'set aside', in contrast to *aposato* in Rom 11:1,
    which the context shows is concerned with rejection.

## Chapter Nineteen

1   See also Jer 24:4–7.
2   A similar pattern is found in Isaiah 11, which speaks of the Spirit
    Yahweh resting on 'a shoot from the stump of Jesse' (11:1), and
    later promises the reassembly of the dispersed exiles (11:12).
3   See also Jer 7:23; 11:4; 30:22; 31:1; 32:38; Ezek 11:20; 36:28;
    37:23, 27.
4   Compare also Rev 21:22–23 and 22:5 with Isa 60:19–20.
5   This connection has added significance in this age of ecological
    concern.

## Chapter Twenty

1   See also Jer 23:5; 33:15; Zech 3:8; 6:12.
2   Some add the rediscovery of divine healing in the nineteenth
    century.
3   The concepts of Catholic substance and Protestant principle
    are taken from Jaroslav Pelikan's *Obedient Rebels: Catholic
    Substance and Protestant Principle in Luther's Reformation* (New
    York & Evanston, Harper & Row, 1964). Pelikan acknowledges
    that he learned them from Paul Tillich.
4   This is not true of the Orthodox Churches, for reasons hinted at
    in the Introduction.

## Chapter Twenty-One

1   From the prayer *Libera nos* following the Our Father.

## Chapter Twenty-Two

1   I use the word 'extra-ordinary' deliberately to convey two ideas:
    first, that the 'new' churches represent God working outside the

'ordinary' structures and secondly in the sense of the size of the phenomenon and thus of God's grace within it.
2  In the United States, the Messianic Jewish Alliance of America plays a significant role of co-ordination and service, but it does not embrace all groups.

## Chapter Twenty-Three

1  See especially Chapter Thirteen.
2  This point was made very clearly in asserting the necessity of the charismatic and the institutional, in the inspiring address of Fr Raniero Cantalamessa at the Brighton Conference in 1991: 'the Spirit precedes, the institution must necessarily follow' (printed in *Good News* 96 (Nov/Dec 1991) p. 6.

## Chapter Twenty-Five

1  The Free Church pattern also applies to the churches of the 'Radical Reformation' that adopted an Anabaptist doctrine and practice. The new churches are the most recent instance of this form of voluntary association.
2  This twofold work of the Spirit is examined in more detail in Chapters Eight and Nine of *One Lord One Spirit One Body*.